AF693961

PRACTICE POINTS FOR TRIAL LAWYERS

A View from Both Sides of the Bench

Judge Mark A. Drummond

LAW LIBRARY
AUG 2 7 2015
GOLDEN GATE UNIVERSITY

AMERICAN BAR ASSOCIATION
Section of Litigation

Cover design by Andrew Alcala/ABA Publishing.

The materials contained herein represent the opinions of the authors and/or the editors, and should not be construed to be the views or opinions of the law firms or companies with whom such persons are in partnership with, associated with, or employed by, nor of the American Bar Association or the Section of Litigation unless adopted pursuant to the bylaws of the Association.

Nothing contained in this book is to be considered as the rendering of legal advice for specific cases, and readers are responsible for obtaining such advice from their own legal counsel. This book is intended for educational and informational purposes only.

© 2015 American Bar Association. All rights reserved.

No part of this publication may be reproduced, stored in a retrieval system, or transmitted in any form or by any means, electronic, mechanical, photocopying, recording, or otherwise, without the prior written permission of the publisher. For permission contact the ABA Copyrights & Contracts Department, copyright@americanbar.org, or complete the online form at http://www.americanbar.org/utility/reprint.html.

Printed in the United States of America.

19 18 17 16 15 5 4 3 2 1

ISBN: 978-1-63425-228-7

e-ISBN: 978-1-63425-229-4

Library of Congress Cataloging-in-Publication Data

Drummond, Mark A., author.
 Practice points for trial lawyers : a view from both sides of the bench / By The Hon. Mark A. Drummond.
 pages cm
 Includes index.
 ISBN 978-1-63425-228-7 (alk. paper)
 1. Trial practice--United States. I. Title.
 KF8915.D78 2015
 347.73'075--dc23

2015027504

Discounts are available for books ordered in bulk. Special consideration is given to state bars, CLE programs, and other bar-related organizations. Inquire at Book Publishing, ABA Publishing, American Bar Association, 321 N. Clark Street, Chicago, Illinois 60654-7598.

www.ShopABA.org

CONTENTS

PREFACE

For me, the most excruciatingly intense period of time is that brief period where the foreperson hands the verdict to the bailiff, who hands it to the judge, who hands it to the clerk to read. All of the months and years of education, training, and preparation are crystalized into that one unique point in time. For a trial attorney, it is the ultimate high—or the ultimate low.

I spent 20 years in front of the bench trying cases. For 15 years I have been on the bench watching cases being tried, and for 30 years I have trained advocates from Tasmania to Tanzania, from Boston to Beijing. I don't know when exactly I started writing the Practice Points column for *Litigation News*, but I was honored when someone in the Section of Litigation thought there were enough columns to justify this book.

After reading these columns one more time before publication, I can tell you that I doubt there is a single, original thought in any of the columns. What I have written comes from my years of trial and error combined with stealing every good technique I saw in court. I have stolen liberally from my fellow trainers at the National Institute for Trial Advocacy.

This book is dedicated to my family—my parents, Gary and Norma, who set an example that I am still trying to achieve; my wife, Carol and our children, David, Alexander, and Jane. They carried on while I was away in trial or teaching.

This book is also dedicated to my mentor, David M. Malone. In 1985, I was one of his students at the National Session of the National Institute for Trial Advocacy held in Boulder, Colorado. He was my team leader. The next year Dave asked me to teach with him. To say that Dave asking me to teach with him changed my life would be a gross understatement. I have taught with, and learned from, some of the greatest trial lawyers in the world, and have traveled the world, due to his taking a chance on me. Dave passed away much too soon, and the world of advocacy training lost one of its stars.

All of the instructors for the National Institute for Trial Advocacy have freely shared their techniques, tips, and tactics with me. It is in this same spirit that I shared them with you through my columns, which are now collected here.

Mark A. Drummond

ABOUT THE AUTHOR

Mark A. Drummond was a trial lawyer for nearly 20 years before taking the bench in 1999. He handled a wide variety of cases including antitrust, trade secrets, products liability, medical malpractice, criminal, divorce, and his brother-in-law's rent case.

His current call consists of exclusively jury and bench trials. He is a Circuit Judge for the Eighth Judicial Circuit of Illinois.

He has been an instructor with the National Institute for Trial Advocacy (NITA) since 1986. He has taught trial advocacy skills for both large and small firms, corporations, the United Nations, the U.S. Department of Justice, the Attorney General's offices for Illinois and New York, and the Department of the Navy. He received the Hon. Robert E. Keeton Faculty Award from NITA in 2008. He teaches future NITA instructors at both training sites in the United States. He is the program director for NITA Teacher Training in New York City.

He is the author of "The Eight Keys to the Art of Persuasion," his one-day trial advocacy program. He writes the "Practice Points" column for *Litigation News* for the Section of Litigation of the American Bar Association.

He has trained judges in presentation skills for the Administrative Office of the Illinois Courts for judges who lecture at the Education Conference and New Judge Seminar. He has trained over 200 judges on how to present his anti-drug and alcohol program for schools, "The Seven Reasons to Leave the Party." This program has been presented since 2008 to over 150,000 students throughout the State of Illinois. In 2009, the presentation was awarded the Special Merit Citation from the American Judicature Society.

His pro bono trial advocacy work includes the NITA and ABA legal services training in Austin, Kansas City, St. Louis, Miami, New Orleans, Jackson, Mississippi, San Francisco, Baltimore, Albuquerque, Columbus, Ohio, and Chicago, training the lay advocates for the Navajo Nation, and training the Bosnian and Rwandan war crimes tribunal prosecutors for the United Nations at Oxford, in the Hague, and in Arusha, Tanzania.

He traveled to Japan in 2008 to train attorneys in jury trial advocacy in advance of their adoption of jury trials in criminal cases. He has trained advocates in Kosovo and Macedonia for the U.S. Department of Justice. He has trained barristers at the Inner Temple in London on techniques on making evidence visual and trained barristers at the Middle Temple on general advocacy skills. He has taught advocacy techniques in Austria, Tasmania, Switzerland, Beijing, Shanghai, and the new LLM course in advocacy at the University of Strathclyde. He regularly teaches barristers at the Keble Course held at Oxford University.

He can be reached at mdrummond@co.adams.il.us or (217) 430-7459.

CHAPTER 1

TRIAL PREPARATION

The Trial Notebook: Nuts and Bolts of Trial Preparation

I cannot give you his name. He would be upset with me. He is considered by his peers to be one of the top trial lawyers in the country. These days, he does not need publicity. Nearly all of his cases now come from other lawyers. He just lets his verdicts do the talking.

He is very talented, very quick and gifted in speech, but when asked the secret to his success, he gives credit to the now-deceased named partner in his firm. He tells others who seek the secret that his mentor may not have had the most astute legal mind, been the greatest orator, or the sharpest cross-examiner. However, he did have one thing over nearly all of his opponents. He was the most prepared person in the courtroom.

He not only knew his case but he also knew how he would try the case if on the other side. He became a legend for being prepared and for winning—and when you combine preparation with talent—watch out.

Great preparation begins with your trial notebook. You should be assembling your trial notebook from the day you file or receive the complaint. The effect of assembling from day one is that you always have the endgame in mind. This focuses you in a way that is different from the settlement mindset. Your case may very well settle for the benefit of your client because you have convinced the other side from day one that you are actually getting ready to try the case.

Take your favorite three-ring binder and make all of the tabs for the sections listed in the following paragraphs.

Start with the cover. I used a binder with a clear plastic sheet on the front and back. Slip the cover into the plastic sheet with the following on it:

- a caption at the top;
- the words "Trial Notebook" in large, bold letters in the middle; and
- your name, address, and contact information at the bottom.

Why do this? You do this so that everyone—opposing counsel, opposing party, your client, the motion judge, and the trial judge—knows that you are preparing for trial. In every case, the other side is evaluating you on two fronts. First, whether you are willing to go to trial and, second, whether you would be any good at it. Your trial notebook sends that message. This is the psychological effect of the notebook. What is the practical effect? The practical effect is that it lessens stress and increases competence. Being fully prepared lets your talent shine through. Not having to worry about finding this, that, or the other thing frees you to listen and think while under the stress of trial.

"I believe at the front of your trial notebook is a 'to do' list," says Eileen M. Letts, Chicago, who served as cochair of the ABA Section of Litigation's Elevating Your Game Task Force and member of the Section's Diversity and Inclusion Committee. "Things are always coming up both before and during the trial, and you need one place to organize everything you have to do."

"I always have an introduction page where I write notes to myself and where I state the case theme," adds Paul Mark Sandler, Baltimore, cochair of the Section's Litigation Institute for Trial Training. "This helps me keep a steady course throughout the case."

From this point on, you can organize the sections as you see fit. "You may want to use more than one notebook, and as many as you desire, such as one for each witness," says Sandler.

You will want a pleadings section. This has the last version of the complaint and answer and any relevant prior pleadings. You will need the pleadings for jury instructions and for motions to conform to the proof. Having them right there prevents you from scrambling through a court file looking for the third amended answer to the fourth amended complaint. Have your motions for directed verdict ready to go in this section.

You need a timeline of both the events in the case and the litigation. It is crucial for you to be able to find dates quickly. Let's say the other side tries to spring a new document on you at trial. If you not only have the dates discovery was sent but also know the number of days between compliance, your objection could go something like this:

> Your honor, we sent a request for production on March 1, the production was due on March 29; 37 days after the due date we received the response. This document was not in that response. On September 15, we sent a request to supplement. We received their response 56 days later—7 days after we had to file a motion to compel. This document was not produced.

How impressive is that? Having the dates at the ready allows you to make this argument. You also need a timeline of the events as they occurred before the lawsuit. Only by putting together a chronology will you be able to see the events as they unfolded. Sometimes, the timing of the event can be just as crucial as the event itself.

Next, the judge will ask you for a statement of the case to read to the jury. Have that ready. Watching two lawyers try to craft an agreeable statement of the case while the jury is waiting tells me they are not really ready for trial. Give the statement of the case to the other attorney early in the case and watch the reaction.

You need a list of witnesses for the same reasons you need the statement of the case. "You need to have a contact list for all witnesses with multiple ways to reach them," counsels Letts. "If a witness fails to appear, you need to have copies of served subpoenas."

An often-underutilized tool available to the trial lawyer is the request to admit facts and genuineness of documents. This simple device helps narrow the issues and gets exhibits admitted without having to mark them, show them to opposing counsel, ask for permission to approach, lay the foundation, and move for their admission. It was always my goal in every trial never to have to lay the foundation for an exhibit in front of a jury unless the foundation, separate and apart from the exhibit, helped my case.

You need a voir dire chart with boxes for alternates. You don't want to be sitting at your table hurriedly creating the jury chart with your pen and the spine of the closest law book.

The trial notebook system that I used involved four notebooks. I had my notebook, which contained all of the elements of the trial notebook, and I had notebooks for the judge, the opposing counsel, and the witness, which contained only the exhibits. This trial notebook system eliminates the exhibit dance; everyone is on the same page, and you can simply direct the witness to a page in his notebook to view an exhibit. Simultaneously with the witness turning to that exhibit, the exhibit is shown on a screen so that jurors are also on the same page.

Your copy of the trial notebook contains your voir dire, opening, closing, and witness examination outlines. The examination outlines have references to exhibits, page and line numbers in depositions, and statements that you will need to impeach or refresh recollection. You need a section for relevant discovery responses, such as requests for production and interrogatories.

The quickest way to aggravate a trial judge is to not have your jury instructions ready. We love those attorneys who have their instructions ready. They have them early, with alternate instructions depending on the proof, and have someone standing by to retype instructions if needed. There is nothing more frustrating than having a group of jurors waiting because we can't get our instructions right.

Have memorandums of law ready. You should anticipate possible evidentiary hurdles. You may be trying a case where you know the law in that area better than the judge. It is one thing for an attorney to argue a point of law based upon recollection. It is quite another when the attorney backs it up with a brief memorandum of law on the point. There is nothing more impressive.

Trial is the ultimate theater. But unlike the theater, the script is not set; it is fluid. Your trial notebook helps you to control the script as it is literally being written in the courtroom, and it helps you write the ending that your client wants.

Tigar on Trials . . . and Life: Information, Instruction, and Inspiration

For my work with the Section of Litigation's Litigation Institute for Trial Training (LITT) and the National Institute for Trial Advocacy (NITA), I read most of the books coming out on advocacy. Some I like, some I really like, and some I do not like. It is a waste of my time to write about books I don't like and, more importantly, a waste of your time to read about a book I don't like. Although reading a really bad book can be as fun as watching a really bad movie, I believe my role is to give you tips as opposed to titters.

Michael E. Tigar's 2009 book, *Nine Principles of Litigation and Life,* is a perfect blend of information, instruction, and inspiration. Tigar—a nationally known trial lawyer, former chair of the Section of Litigation, and Professor Emeritus of Law at Duke Law School—covers the trial waterfront from Adams to Zenger (that is, John and John Peter, respectively) in 290 pages arranged in a unique and compelling format.

Most books on trial advocacy organize the topics in chronological order, starting with voir dire and ending with closing argument. Tigar organizes his book on advocacy around nine core principles.

Nine Principles of Litigation and Life

Courage
Rapport
Skepticism
Observation
Preparation
Structure

Candor
Empowerment
Presentation

"As I thought about the process of getting ready for trial it seemed to me that it would be helpful to organize the materials along a different set of principles rather than opening statement, direct examination, cross-examination, and so on," says Tigar. "I wanted to talk about the process as it is experienced by lawyers sitting in their offices."

In his preface, Tigar readily admits that he has borrowed from his other books in addition to sharing what other advocates have done. He gives the reader a "Litigator's Bookshelf" and tells where to find those books. Each chapter is divided into subchapters, which support one of the nine principles. An added benefit is a "Notes" section at the end of each chapter, packed with reference material.

Taking a counterintuitive approach, Tigar's last chapter is "Presentation." "I put presentation last because more than 90% of our cases are settled," says Tigar, "I wanted to start with the qualities you should exhibit when the client comes in the door." He begins with courage.

C.S. Lewis once wrote, "Courage is not simply one of the virtues but the form of every virtue at the testing point . . . ." Tigar begins with several types of courage but at the core of this chapter is a subchapter on the courage to go to trial. After trying cases for two decades and settling cases as a judge for a decade, I can tell you with near certainty those attorneys who will put it on the line and those who will not. More importantly, all of the other lawyers know it too. Tigar argues that going to trial benefits particular clients, certainly the lawyers who lay it on the line, and the system in general. But how does the young lawyer find cases to try?

"From the first moment that I started in law practice I let the world know that I was available to get appointed," advises Tigar. "There are all sorts of opportunities to get out there and be involved in litigation. If you look at the world out there, I don't think it can be said that the world is over-lawyered. There are many, many people that cannot afford representation, do not get representation. There are criminal defendants every day who are pleading guilty to things who really have triable cases, consumers who are defrauded that have claims that they do not know how to bring, and there are legal services' offices. It is a question of being available."

In addition to the courage to go to trial, Tigar shares tales of courage to stand up to the judge, to juror prejudice, and to the public, media, and colleagues. He gives specific advice on ways of dealing with these thorny issues, and advice from him and others who have been there. Perhaps most valuable are his tips on dealing with difficult judges without sacrificing your client, your reputation, or the case.

Working from the broad base of courage, Tigar then explores the principle of "Rapport" with clients, judges, and jurors. Included in this chapter is a particularly revealing and complete newspaper article from the *Daily Oklahoman* on Tigar's voir dire techniques in the Terry Nichols's case. He weaves the reporter's story of the jury selection with bracketed notes of advice from him and others. One might think the jury selection in the Nichols's case was very fact specific, but the techniques apply to jury selection in any case.

He then moves to "Skepticism." He develops themes on developing a healthy skepticism in the minds of jurors and judges to wait until they hear all sides before jumping to a conclusion. He explores the use of realistic skepticism when testing your own client's case and the needed skepticism when dealing with your adversary.

From that, he moves to "Observation." Borrowing from Monet, he links trial lawyers to the impressionist painters. Memories fade, events are recalled differently by the witnesses, and it is up to the trial lawyer to paint the canvas to give the jury the correct "impression" of what actually happened. To organize the "impression" you want to make, he then takes you to "Preparation."

"You cannot advantageously settle a case that you are not prepared to try, because you simply are not credible," advises Tigar. "The first criminal case I ever tried was against Bob Bennett, the U.S. attorney. Well, I don't know how many cases he had, but for me, it was a learning experience, so I prepared five times as much as he did and I ended up winning the case."

In "Preparation," Tigar gives the reader a nuts and bolts primer on three documents essential for each case: chronology, who's who, and exhibits.

It is so nuts and bolts that he shares his preferred format for printing and the font size he likes best for these tools.

He then lists the components of an oral argument notebook. Unless you are looking to reinvent the wheel, years of trial and error can be avoided through using the tips in this chapter.

"Preparation" then segues into the "Structure" chapter, which addresses that broad topic as applied to legal and evidence rules, your trial team, case plan, courtroom space, opening, direct and cross, and closing. From the brass tacks recipes contained in "Preparation" and "Structure," he moves to the more intangible, but just as important, principle of "Candor."

"A reputation of a thousand years may depend upon the conduct of a single moment," said the English author Ernest Bramah. In his chapter on "Candor," Tigar addresses how to build and maintain that most valuable of commodities—your word.

He addresses your candor with the judge and with the jury and tips on your client's and your witnesses' candor in court.

Next comes "Empowerment." Those who have never tried a jury case and those who try jury case after jury case (usually only state's attorneys and public defenders) never know, or can lose sight of, really how alien the process can be for jurors. The day before their jury service, they were mowing lawns, paying bills, and transporting children. We rip them out of their homes, place them in large wooden boxes, and make them answer questions about their lives in front of perhaps a hundred other people. Tigar gives concrete examples of how to build bridges to the jurors and empower them to make the right decision.

Finally, Tigar gives us "Presentation." As Tigar notes, this is the shortest chapter. In it, he gives the reader his "Revised Standard Ten Commandments of Cross-Examination—and Direct As Well." He tells us that it is the shortest chapter because so much of the groundwork has been laid if the attorney will just follow the previous eight principles.

In closing, I want to comment on something that I have never commented on before—price. At the risk of you thinking I am working on commission (I am not), I must tell you that the cost of this book is remarkably low given the value between its covers and when compared to some of its lesser brethren. I will tell you that Tigar's tip on the follow-up question to ask when a juror begins a response as to whether they can keep an open mind or disregard irrelevant matters with "I think I can . . ." is worth the price of the book alone.

Resources:

Michael E. Tigar, *Nine Principles of Litigation and Life* (ABA 2009). Available from the ABA Web Store at www.ababooks.org or 1-800-285-2221.

C.S. Lewis, "Letter 29," *The Screwtape Letters* (1942).

Working Backward from the Appeal

"The events recounted in this opinion show that [he] is a menace to his clients and a scofflaw with respect to appellate procedure." The attorney was reprimanded, fined $5,000, and ordered to send his clients "copies of this opinion so that they may consider whether to file malpractice suits against him." Wow.

The attorney represented three employees of the Cook County prison system. They claimed their employer discriminated against black workers when making promotions. In affirming a dismissal based on a statute of limitations, the U.S. Court of Appeals for the Seventh Circuit concluded that both counsel and the lower court were in error on the law.

The plaintiffs are left with either a long shot at the U.S. Supreme Court or a malpractice action. As far as the attorney goes, the opinion illustrates the extreme end of the bell curve of what not to do.

So, what is the other end of the bell curve? At the risk of stereotyping, I think both attorneys and judges can be divided into three broad categories. The first are those attorneys and judges who have the luxury of working in a very narrow area of the law. They are the specialists. They handle one type of case and one type of case only for many years, and it is relatively easy for them to keep on top of new developments.

In the second category are attorneys and judges who have been practicing or hearing a variety of cases for a very long time. They are not specialists. They rely totally on experience or what happened in their last case of this type. They rarely make the effort to see if that pesky thing known as "the law" has changed.

Attorneys and judges in this second group tend to cite themselves or their experience as authority. Other attorneys seem to defer to them solely due to the number of years they have practiced. Although I wish I were a savant when it comes to law, I am not. I cannot count the number of times I have admitted my ignorance on a point of law and have asked the attorneys if they had any law to give me. This request is sometimes met with blank stares and a half-hearted offer to look something up if I think it is "necessary."

It is necessary.

Those in the third group are also generalists. They are the trial lawyers who try a wide variety of cases. They are the trial judges who hear a wide variety of cases. But unlike the generalists in the second group, they know that the law changes—sometimes from day to day, from district to district, and from judge to judge.

It is impossible for me, as a trial judge, to be prepared on every single legal point that may come at me. I don't have the one variable in the equation that you do: the evidence. The best trial lawyers know this. No matter how good a judge you have on the bench, he or she may need to be educated on the law as the evidence develops.

Moreover, what the jury or judge may giveth, the appellate court may taketh away. I once wrote that one of the top 10 things that trial judges want is to be affirmed on appeal. I remember each and every reversal. One of my greatest fears is to have to impose on another hundred or so people to come to the courthouse to hear a case a second time due to something I've screwed up.

"Remember every time you are speaking in a courtroom you are speaking to multiple audiences," counsels Nash E. Long III, Charlotte, NC, cochair of the Section of Litigation's Health Law Committee and former cochair of its Trial Practice Committee. "The first is the jury, the second is the judge, and the third is the reviewing court. It is critically important to keep these audiences in mind; to make sure you are protecting the record while communicating with the jury and the judge."

The very best, the attorneys at the far end of the bell curve of competence, tend to work a case backward. They know that until the check is in the bank or the last appeal has been decided, the case is never truly over.

"My appellate practice is split between cases that I see only after a final verdict and those that I participate in at the trial or even pretrial stages," says Thomas J. Donlon, Stamford, CT, cochair of the Section's Amicus

Curiae Briefs Committee and former cochair of its Appellate Practice Committee. "As a matter of preference and good practice, I counsel trial attorneys to follow the wider path and involve me as soon as possible."

"We use appellate lawyers quite frequently as we get ready for trial or even earlier, depending on the case," agrees Long. "We have a group called 'The Appellate and Critical Motions Team,' and, in addition to appeals, they are assigned to assist the trial team in developing key arguments that need to be made and preserved so that nothing is lost or waived."

"The Section's Appellate Practice Committee has presented programs on this very topic," echoes Donlon. "Such involvement allows the appellate specialist to contribute in areas of their expertise—both procedural, such as preservation of issues, and substantive, such as law at motion and summary judgment stages, all while allowing the trial litigator to focus on what they do best—convincing the trier of fact that our client should win."

But what if you are the lone ranger? In a sense, judges are, for the most part, on their own, unless they have the luxury of law clerks. When I don't know the law in a particular area, I find legal search engines invaluable. I simply try to boil the issue down to the smallest number of cases, and then I type "reversed or remanded" and see what pops up.

When I speak at schools, I tell students that one reason we all wear black robes is to convey that you should get the same justice regardless of who wears the robe. We all know, however, that each judge has different training, education, and experiences. You may be in front of a judge who was just given a new assignment, is covering for another judge, or is the only judge in that county and must handle everything from asbestos cases to dogs "running at large" cases.

"In the state system in North Carolina, you might have a different judge at each step of the case and a different judge at trial," says Long. "You may have to be educating about a specific point of law that is narrow or new, but also what has happened before in the very case you are dealing with. I use bench briefs or motions in limine to get these points across."

"For a bench brief, the shorter the better," continues Long. "It is no more than two or three pages long; it is crisply written, focused, and is given to opposing counsel before the day begins."

The topics for a bench brief are limited only by your imagination. Traditionally, they cover evidentiary issues or point of laws. However, they can be used whenever you are concerned that you may need written backup for what you say or simply as an aid to the court. You may want to assist the court with a timeline of significant, uncontested dates or perhaps list of witnesses and where they fit into the case.

As a trial judge, I cannot remember a time when I refused to admit a bench brief. They are always an aid to me. I like having something in writing as opposed to relying totally on my notes, and they help create a record.

For the attorney just starting out, a bench brief shows your client, your opponent, and your judge that you know what you are doing and that you are willing to go the extra mile. This is especially true if you are opposing one of the lions of the trial bar and the judge seems to be deferring to his or her experience.

I am asked frequently how a lawyer, especially a young lawyer, tells a judge that if he or she rules a certain way, the appellate court will reverse. The bench brief helps because it puts in writing the cases that show the judge reversals and remands back to the trial court. I tell young lawyers to approach that rather delicate issue with statements such as, "Your Honor, we feel that if this evidence is admitted, this case may be coming back and we have prepared a bench brief in support of our position."

Trust me, the judge will listen, will take the time to read the brief, and will pay particular attention to the words "reversed" and "remanded." The phrase "this case may be coming back" is powerful. We listen to that. Having a do-over because of our mistake is one of our greatest fears.

Resources:

Lee v. Cook County, Ill., 635 F.3d 969 (7th Cir. 2011).

Susan J. Irion, "How to Deal Like a Professional with Adverse Legal Authority," *Litigation* (Winter 2011, ABA).

Mary-Christine Sungaila, "What Appellate Lawyers Should Know about Making a Trial Record," *App. Prac. J.*, Winter 2011, *available at* apps.americanbar.org/litigation/committees/appellate/newsletter.html.

Mark A. Drummond, "What Judges Want," *Litigation* (Summer 2005, ABA).

Know Thy Judge

You wouldn't think about waiving voir dire in a jury trial, would you? But how do you voir dire a judge? You should want to know as much as possible about the person you are trying to persuade. So how do you, within the bounds of ethics, find out about the judge and what can you do once you find out? The first step is to find out which judge is assigned to your case and to realize that you may have options. Some states, such as Illinois, allow counsel to seek a change of judge without alleging any bias whatsoever, provided the judge has not ruled on any matters of substance.

When speaking to students, I am sometimes asked why judges all wear black robes. My answer is that judges want to convey that they are all the same. However, they are not. All judges are the same in terms of wanting to reach a just result, but they may arrive at that destination by different paths, with different procedures. Each judge is shaped by his or her education, training, and experience. To ignore this is to ignore human nature and reality. So how do you find out about your judge? Here are 10 ways.

1. Call the Judge

Some judges have their preferred procedures written out for distribution to counsel. If they don't, in my opinion, there is absolutely nothing improper about an attorney asking, "Judge, I've never tried a case in front of you. Do you have any procedures that I should know about before I come to your court?"

2. Call Other Lawyers

There's an old joke about an older lawyer asking a younger lawyer if he knew the translation of every Latin phrase that appears above every courthouse in the United States. The punchline: Regardless of the actual translation, they all say: "Hire local counsel." "I try to tap into a small organization of local lawyers," says Lorna G. Schofield, New York, past

Chair of the ABA Section of Litigation. "For example, in New York City, the New York Council of Defense Lawyers allows group posts. If someone has something informative and sensitive to say, they generally suggest a phone call. If I'm out of my home town, I ask my local counsel to tap into any similar grapevine," Schofield says.

3. Type the Judge's Name into a Legal Search Engine

Doing an Internet search should give you the judge's opinions, if they have been appealed, but can also give you opinions on cases that the judge tried while practicing law. This is priceless insight into how that particular judge approaches a particular issue.

4. Check Past Attorney Directories and Current Judicial Directories

Past attorney directories will give you the judge's area of practice before taking the bench. It is good to know if judges specialized in one area their entire career or on one side—plaintiff/prosecution or defense—for their entire career. What organizations did they belong to as lawyers; what honors were given? Current judicial directories can tell you whether a state court judge was appointed or elected and when he or she is scheduled for reappointment or reelection. Would you really want to have a sentencing hearing where you are going to ask the judge to take a chance on your career criminal and give him probation, instead of prison, the week before the judge is on the ballot? Having this information in a case that you know is going to make the papers may prompt you to ask for a sentencing date after the election. That may be best for your client and a relief to the judge.

Judicial directories can also show you the judge's current and past assignments as well as how long he or she has been on the bench. In my experience, judges who practiced for a substantial period of time before they took the bench are, with some exceptions, the best trial judges. They understand the demands of being a trial lawyer. In an ideal world, all judges would hit the bench running, having an encyclopedic knowledge of both the law of evidence and the law applicable to their particular assignment. But, because this is not necessarily the case, find out if you will need to educate the judge in a particular field.

5. Check Local Newspapers

Many local newspapers have a day on which they publish activities of people in the local community. Some judges embrace publicity; some judges avoid it. There are some professionals who submit their attendance at any conference or seminar, however obscure it may be, to the local newspaper. If you are in a high-profile case that will be covered by the media, knowing whether your judge seeks or avoids publicity can be valuable.

6. Talk to Court Reporters

"I always try to obtain a transcript of a recent trial," says Steven D. Susman, Houston, Life Fellow of the Section of Litigation. "You can tell what the judge wants, doesn't want, how he or she conducts the trial and rules on objections. Most court reporters are happy to sell you whatever you want and also point you to the right transcript," Susman advises.

7. Google the Judge

This should give you everything else that is not covered by the legal search engines. It is truly amazing what is on the Internet that can be of value to the trial attorney.

8. Go to Court

While transcripts can be read quickly, without having to take the time to sit through a trial, what if there's no time to get a transcript? "Go sit in the judge's courtroom when she or he does a motion call," advises Mark A. Neubauer, Los Angeles, Life Fellow and Division II Director of the Section. "A trial doesn't have enough action by the judge; a law and motion calendar shows the judge in rapid fire. You can learn a lot by watching how the judge handles different matters and different attorneys. In short, you get a feel for your audience by watching the judge at work," Neubauer says.

9. Talk to Present and Former Law Clerks

Former law clerks can be a great resource in learning about the procedures of the judge and any particular idiosyncrasies that the judge may have with regard to trials, exhibits, courtroom conduct, etc.

10. Befriend Courtroom Personnel

One veteran trial lawyer once told me to show up at least a half or a full hour before trial. He told me that he learned volumes from off-hand comments, overheard comments, or comments made directly to him by courtroom personnel. He was one of the most well-liked attorneys by courthouse personnel. The things he learned simply by showing up early and listening were amazing. Remember, the bailiffs, clerks, and court reporters have had years of experience sitting in court with a variety of different judges. They know if the judge always requires that counsel stand, whether you must ask each time to approach the witness or the bench, and even the judge's position on gum! For some judges, gum in a witness's mouth is a cardinal sin that must be exorcised before the witness testifies. The last thing you want in your trial is for the judge to hand your star witness a tissue so he or she can spit the gum out before testifying. It tends to ruin the moment.

Resource:

"Resources Useful for Locating Judicial Clerkships and Researching Judges," *available at* http://law.wisc.edu/career/PrintResources.htm.

What Judges Want

Before I launch into this I want you to know that as a trial lawyer I violated most of these rules—sometimes in the same trial! But after trying cases for twenty years, and being a trial judge for six, I think I can reduce what judges want down to a top ten list.

1. We Want the Exhibit

Since judges are individuals, each has idiosyncrasies. There are some judges that have so many idiosyncrasies they feel it necessary to have written rules for the lawyers to follow in their courtroom. Although the lawyers in my court may tell you something different, I believe I have only one idiosyncrasy and here it is: **I want the exhibit! I want to see the exhibit at the same time the lawyer is questioning the witness on the exhibit.**

I applaud attorneys who are trying to save our natural resources, but nothing frustrates me more than what I call "The one exhibit trial." What usually happens is the lawyer has only one exhibit and gives it to the witness. A direct examination is then conducted over the right shoulder of the witness while the other lawyer is standing over the left shoulder to see what they are talking about. The following is an actual exchange that occurred the other day in court:

> Lawyer 1: "Would you read that line of the contract for the court?"
> (Witness reads)
> Lawyer 2: "Objection your honor, rule of completeness."
> Me: "May I see the exhibit?"
> Lawyer 1: "No"
> Me: "Why?"
> Lawyer 1: "I have not introduced it into evidence"

> Me: (slightly exasperated) "Yes, but I'm the one who admits it into evidence."
> Lawyer 1: "Oh."

Did I mention this was a bench trial?

I don't know how many times a lawyer has been examining a witness concerning a multi-part contract, a tax return, or a line-item budget without me having a benefit of a copy. Even if the judge in a former life was a stenographic court reporter, it is simply much easier to follow along with the exhibit in front of you. If you give the judge a courtesy copy, you are more likely to get the correct result for your client in the shortest period of time. I, and many of my fellow judges, keep various colored highlighters and sticky notes on our bench to mark the courtesy copy of the exhibit. For example, I may highlight income in green and deductions in yellow on a tax return. I write questions I want to ask on the exhibit next to the relevant part of the exhibit. There is nothing more frustrating for a judge than not being able to see what everybody else sees in the courtroom.

2. We Want the Law

What is the shortest distance between the doors of your law school and earning the respect of judges? Following Model Rule of Professional Conduct 3.3(a)(2). The rule is:

> A lawyer shall not knowingly fail to disclose to the tribunal authority in the controlling jurisdiction known to the lawyer to be directly adverse to the position of the client and not disclosed by opposing counsel.

In fact, I tell new attorneys to take the words "directly adverse" and change them to "arguably adverse." Why? There is nothing more impressive than the advocate who comes into court and says, for example, "Your honor, this is our position. However, there are three cases that are arguably against us. We have cited those to you, but we believe two of those cases are distinguishable on their facts and one is just bad law. We also have two cases in our favor . . . ."

Judges learn very quickly who they can rely on to tell them the current state of the law. Citing contrary authority builds your reputation as an ethical advocate. For judges who may be dealing with hundreds of files covering myriad legal issues, there is nothing more powerful than being known as the advocate that a judge can always count on for accurate statements as to the law.

There is also a persuasive power to citing contrary authority. It appears that you are less concerned about it when you admit its existence—and it is even more devastating for the other side when you cite cases that are against you that they have not found. No less an advocate than Cicero said that the perfect advocate is one who could argue both sides of any case.

3. We Want Objections That Matter

Judges become frustrated with what I will call "sport objections." A sport objection is an objection made merely for the sport of it. The other day we were at the end of a trial that had to be continued. One of the parties had not shown up in court and I asked the representative of an agency the efforts that had been made to notify the party. The representative started to tell me that the party who was in court had told her that she had called the other party to advise him of the date. There was a hearsay objection. Now the fact that this attorney's client had tried to notify the party of the hearing date didn't make a hill of beans worth of difference to his client's case. In fact, the fact that she took the time and effort to try to call the other party put her in a better light. The opportunity to object does not translate into actually objecting.

Every so often an objection actually hurts your case. In this case, the lawyer who objected wanted the party to be making more money and this exchange occurred:

> Lawyer 1: "Now, do you have any chance to move up in the organization?" (From his vocal intonation, he is assuming the answer is going to be "no.")
> Witness: "Yes, they told me . . ."
> Lawyer 2: "Objection—hearsay!"

> Me: "I would sustain that objection, but the bigger question is why would you object since she started with 'yes.'"
> Lawyer 2: "Objection withdrawn."
> Witness: "Yes, they told me I would be in line for the manager's job which ranges from $40,000 to $60,000 per year." (A factor of two to three times what she was currently earning.)

These are knee-jerk objections. Anytime they hear the word "said" they make a hearsay objection without asking first, "Will this hurt me?" or "Will this help me?" or "Does this matter?"

4. We Want Good Jury Instructions

Lawyers work more hours than judges. Any judge who disagrees is either a rare exception or did not work many hours as an attorney. Therefore, I always try to accommodate the attorneys' schedules and try to save attorneys time. However, there is one group of people whose time I place above the attorneys'. I value the jurors' time more than the attorneys' time.

Nothing frustrates a judge more than having the jury twiddle their thumbs while we try to craft a usable set of jury instructions. Ninety percent of the jury instructions should be completed before trial and given to the judge. Alternate instructions based upon how the evidence may shake out should be typed and ready to go for the instruction conference. If you don't do many jury trials, ask those who have, such as a state's attorneys, how to do this. They will know what I mean.

5. We Want You to Know Us

Most know the Greek maxim "Know thyself." Experienced trial attorneys will tell you "Know thy judge." As I said before, I would like to think that I have only the "The one exhibit trial" pet peeve. However, I know many judges that have more than one pet peeve. I know. You're shocked! How do you ethically find out about the judge? Here are some suggestions:

1. Call the judge—I have no problem with an out-of-town attorney calling me and asking about procedure in my courtroom.

2. Call the judge's clerk—if you feel uncomfortable contacting the judge directly or you know that a particular judge does not want to talk to any attorney without the other attorney being there, even on matters of procedure. Many judge's clerks or secretaries know the procedure.
3. Ask for the written rules—many judges have a list of the procedures they like in their courtroom available to the attorneys.
4. Call another attorney who has tried a case in front of that judge—start off the conversation with, "Hey, I heard you got a good result in the Smith case." And after the attorney talks for about 15 minutes you can say, "Tell me about Judge Jones."

6. We Want to Be Affirmed on Appeal

For the most part, our biggest fear is having a jury trial overturned and having to do it all over again. In a perfect world, every judge would have a law professor's encyclopedic knowledge on the particular area of the law. Some judges do become specialists and have the luxury of knowing everything there is to know about a certain narrow area of the law. However, most of us rotate assignments and, especially in rural counties, the jury trials may be few and far between. I can remember as a practicing attorney a judge thanking me for taking a civil case to jury trial. He had been a judge for eight years in that county and had never heard one civil jury trial case!

If you are taking a jury case to trial, you have probably lived with that case for up to a year or more. Probably the only person in the courtroom who knows as much about the case as you do is opposing counsel. We judges sometimes do not track on why a particular piece of evidence is relevant, and we need time to either digest your argument or have some law on the point.

What do you do? Make liberal use of offers of proof and don't be afraid to ask me to reconsider a prior ruling during a break in the jury trial. An offer of proof made outside the presence of the jury preserves the issue for appeal and also gives me more time to think about it without the pressure of 24 eyes staring at me expecting a split-second decision. I may need time to do some quick research on the law or a particular evidentiary point during the break. Don't assume "objection sustained" is the end of it. I don't want to have to do this again, and if you are an attorney that I can trust on issues of law or evidence, I will always give you a second chance.

7. We Want Civility

I once told a young attorney during a trial training course, "You can't treat every witness as if they were born on this earth for the sole purpose of messing with your case." Some attorneys just can't help themselves and really emphasize the word "cross" in cross-examination. On a couple of occasions when I was practicing, I lost clients to attorneys who the clients thought were more "aggressive." I know that the aggressive attorneys may give the clients a certain dose of psychic gratification, especially in divorce cases, by the use of aggressive tactics. But I can tell you as a judge, and from juror feedback questionnaires, that the people who decide the cases do not appreciate posturing—or, put another way, "the show" — simply to show off for the client.

The question the attorney must ask is whether aggression is persuasive. An example to illustrate my point: the attorney wants to show that the witness (plaintiff) did not seek medical treatment after the accident. The aggressive attorney would do something like this:

> Attorney: "After the accident, you didn't ask for an ambulance?"
> Witness: "Well I didn't feel hurt at that time"
> Attorney: (Loud and dripping with sarcasm) "Ms. Smith, I didn't ask you how you felt, I asked whether you asked for an ambulance. Yes or no. Now can you answer that?"

The contrast is for the attorney to simply repeat the question slower and softer until the attorney gets the answer he or she wants.

> Attorney: "You didn't ask for an ambulance?"
> Witnesses: "Well I didn't feel hurt at that time."
> Attorney: (softer) "You didn't ask for an ambulance?"
> Witness: "Well, like I said I didn't feel hurt at the time."

Attorney: (even softer and slower) "You didn't ask for an ambulance?"
Witness: "No."

By simply repeating the simple question to which the attorney is entitled to a "yes or no" answer, the jury is soon sitting there siding with the attorney and looking at the witness screaming in their minds, "**Oh, just answer the question!**" The longer it takes the witnesses to answer this simple question, the better it is for the attorney. The attorney who uses the non-aggressive technique of repetition shows the jury how the witness is avoiding the question. Attorneys must realize that naked aggression, for the most part, is solely for the gratification of themselves or their client. It rarely persuades the people who count.

8. We Want a Trial Notebook

I have already talked about having the exhibit in front of me. If you really want to impress us—make a trial notebook. The trial notebook system is this: Four notebooks: one for you, opposing counsel, the witness, and the judge. The original exhibits are in the witness's trial notebook. At the front of the trial notebook there can be various items that are useful to the judge. Many of my trial notebooks included the following:

1. a chronology of the case
2. a list of witnesses involved in the case including their titles, if applicable
3. a combined request to admit facts and the response to that request
4. cites to the applicable statutory or case law
5. proposed judgment: on paper and computer disk

In my trial notebook, I would include my opponent's exhibits. Many times my opponents would tell me that we could just use my trial notebook, since it had all the exhibits. What tactical advantage is this? It allowed me to put the exhibits in the order that I wanted the judge to see them. I am not sure this is any great tactical advantage, but in a case that goes to trial which, by definition, should be a close call, you should probably seek any advantage.

The trial notebook system eliminates the exhibit dance in the courtroom. It eliminates the attorney from having to ask permission to approach the witness and from stating for the record that he is now showing the exhibit to opposing counsel and going back to his or her chair. It becomes simply, "Would you please turn to Exhibit 24?" and everyone turns the page. It is so elegant. It is so surgical. It is so persuasive.

9. We Want the Judgment

You might want to ask the judge, with opposing counsel present, whether or not the judge would like the judgment you proposed in an electronic format that the judge could alter as he or she sees fit. I heard of one judge who took this to the extreme. He would have both attorneys prepare a judgment and he would sign whichever one he agreed with—no additions, no corrections, no deletions—or so legend has it.

There is certainly nothing improper saying to the judge at the end of your closing argument, "Your honor, this is our position in the case and for your convenience I have drafted an order citing the underlying law that we believe is applicable, certain findings of fact and reflecting a judgment based upon our argument on this computer disk and I will also give a copy to counsel." If a judge practices in a particular area for any length of time, he or she probably has a skeleton form on their computer that they use all the time. However, if you are in front of a judge who deals with many cases or is on special assignment, providing a copy of a proposed judgment in an electronic format, which he or she can change, is a real help.

10. We Want to Talk about the Cases

The problem is we can't. In some of the counties in our circuit, there is only one judge. It must be lonely. I have the benefit of being able to talk to six other judges in my courthouse about cases. We would really love to be able to talk to the attorneys about the cases, but it becomes a slippery slope. The only time we could possibly talk to the attorneys is after any appeals have been exhausted, yet we are still concerned about post-judgment matters. Most of us loved being trial attorneys, so not being able to talk to attorneys about particular cases, particular witnesses, or particular strategies is the biggest loss for us in taking the bench.

So after we retire, regale us with stories. Until then, we former trial lawyers must live vicariously. Good luck.

CHAPTER 2

JURY SELECTION

Bloggers, Bailouts, and the Economy

It is early. The sun is barely peeking over the horizon. You are in your car with the radio on. In about two hours, you will start selecting a jury in your client's personal injury case. The news is on and things haven't changed. Unemployment is still hovering around 15 percent in your area. The average wait between jobs is still 18 months.

Your client's injuries kept her out of work for a month. Her medical bills were $20,000, but she makes $150,000 a year working for a well-known financial institution that has been in the paper after they received $100 million in the federal bailout.

You pull up to the courthouse and walk through a throng of people who are probably jurors. Most are on their phone, talking, texting, or just staring at the screen. You ask yourself whether you would want a juror who was laid off from a job that paid $60,000 a year, was out of work for nine months, and is now only working part-time at a minimum-wage job.

The landscape has changed. Jury pools are filled with people who are unemployed or have been downsized. If you represent a big company, jurors have instant access to whether your company was bailed out and how much the chief executive earns per year. Any juror can type your name or your client's name into a search engine and start reading.

A 2010 article in the *Los Angeles Times* told of a case in which 66 out of 107 potential jurors were excused due to financial difficulties. The same article told of a sheriff's deputy suing his former sergeant for allegedly causing severe emotional distress due to lewd and false innuendos that he was gay. Two jurors had tried to get dismissed on financial hardship grounds and were unsuccessful.

However, they did succeed when one said, "He's brave enough to go out and get shot at by anyone, but he couldn't handle this?" and the other added, "I think severe emotional distress is what is happening in Haiti. I don't think you could have such severe emotional distress from that."

The dismissal of these two jurors emboldened others and, after three days, both lawyers agreed to waive a jury and leave the decision up to the judge.

"Juror distractions are immense these days," says Dr. Jo-Ellan Dimitrius, Pasadena, CA, nationally known jury consultant and a speaker for the ABA Section of Litigation's Litigation Institute for Trial Training. "With double digit unemployment, we have seen everything from jurors asking if their jury pay would affect their unemployment, to emotional outbursts, to almost rebellion," Dimitrius says.

"What I have seen, which is just remarkable to me, is that the judge will go through all the hardship issues. Then, when they are about to be sworn, all of a sudden, six hands will go up and the people will say they cannot serve due to loss of jobs or benefits," Dimitrius says.

"I am suggesting to attorneys that they have a pretrial conference with the judge addressing these issues, particularly if it is a long, protracted trial," counsels Dimitrius. "In the past two years, I have seen jurors become much more emboldened to challenge judges on these financial issues to the point of screaming at the judge that they can't make their mortgage payment. My advice to attorneys is to ask themselves if they really want a juror who is so concerned about their personal life that the juror either holds it against them or their client or the juror simply does not pay attention to the case. I just read that more than one quarter of all jurors in Los Angeles County were released on hardship grounds just this past year."

"This results in jury pools that are skewed toward retirees and government workers and sometimes demographics are a factor," adds Dimitrius. "Take a toxic tort case where, historically, the defense wants older jurors who remember the days that you could go and dump out oil, while the plaintiffs want younger persons who might have a more 'green' perspective."

"Our research has revealed that people who perceive themselves as victims or are financially distressed, tend to identify with the 'little guy,'" says jury consultant Dr. Samantha D. Holmes, Houston.

"I tell attorneys not to pick one single item, such as age, income level, or employment status as the measure of whether they are going to be a good or bad juror. The two most important factors are any attitudes toward the particular type of case being tried and how they view their life," she advises.

"If you have a person who believes they are not being appreciated, or are underemployed or angry about their lot in life, they are generally going to be plaintiff-oriented folks," continues Holmes. "People who are happy in their life or accept where they are in life, whether or not they are highly educated or have a lot of money, are usually more willing to listen to the defense story," Holmes says.

Over the past few years, millions of Americans who never missed a credit card payment have had their interest rates increase, credit lines lowered, and cards cancelled. Websites abound that list financial institutions that got bailed out along with the salaries of CEOs of failed businesses. Wall Street versus Main Street is the perennial debate between politicians. What if your client falls into the catchall category of "big business"?

"As in most corporate cases, it's especially important to make the case about people and humanize the situation," says Hon. Lorna G. Schofield, New York City, U.S. District Judge for the Southern District of New York and past Section Chair. "First, the corporation has to be humanized," agrees Dimitrius. "Second, we as consultants are, more and more, being brought in at relatively early stages to assess the venue's attitudes toward that particular institution."

"I routinely engage a jury consultant before trials," advises Paul Mark Sandler, Baltimore, cochair of the Section's Litigation Institute for Trial Training. "We conduct a mock trial composed of citizens in the community that the consultant and the trial team consider to match the profile of the prospective jury pool. The jury consultant selects the jury from lists available in various consultant agencies that conduct focus groups for businesses."

"One relatively new thing for the legal community is the Internet survey," suggests Dimitrius. "Phone surveys may cost $50,000, $60,000 or $70,000 and are now are less effective with the advent of caller ID, whereas an Internet survey can be done anywhere from $5,000 to $20,000," Dimitrius says.

"Early on, we can use it to determine bias, level of knowledge about a particular case, or use it for profiling purposes as the case gets closer to trial. It is about 75 percent cheaper and about 75 percent faster than phone surveys, and we can evaluate the data in real time," Dimitrius notes.

Finally, one of all judges' greatest fears is having a jury case reversed because we have failed to control access to electronic information. Cases are being reversed due to jurors doing independent research or blogging about cases.

"There are sites, such as Technorati, that will search for blogs," says Dimitrius. "As a matter of practice, we will now Google, Technorati, and Myspace, if you will, the prospective jurors to find out anything we can, apart from what they have shared in the voir dire process. I was just reading about an attorney asking for a new trial in a murder case in Fresno County where a judge was sending emails to fellow judges about the case while he was sitting as a juror in the murder case."

"Both the judge and the attorneys need to be ever vigilant that a juror may be blogging about the case," advises Dimitrius. "One plaintiff's attorney I know has his staff check every day to see if any juror is blogging about the case, and I tell attorneys they need to be proactive in pretrial conferences in bringing this to the attention of the trial judge."

Courts throughout the United States are drafting new rules governing the use of electronic devices in courthouses and jury instructions prohibiting communication about the case through electronic media.

As a final note of caution, if you are checking out the jurors, remember the reverse can also happen. Do you have a website, social or professional networking page, or do you Tweet? If so, ask yourself if your message on the Internet is the same message you are sending in court.

Resources:

Deborah Cassens Weiss, "'Scary' Jurors Spur Switch to Bench Trial Highlighting Growing Problem", *ABA J.* (Feb. 16, 2010), *available at* www.abajournal.com.

Deborah Cassens Weiss, "Jurors' Wikipedia Research, Friending at Issue in Two Md. Cases", *ABA J.* (Dec. 14, 2009), *available at* www.abajournal.com.

Carol J. Williams, "Weighed Down by Recession Woes, Jurors Are Becoming Disgruntled", *LA Times* (Feb. 15, 2010).

Paul W. Grimm, Charles S. Fax & Paul Mark Sandler, *Discovery Problems and Their Solutions*, Second Edition, Chapter 27-"Discovery of Jury Consultant, Focus Group Materials, and Related Communications" (ABA 2009), available from the ABA Web Store at www.ababooks .org or call 1-800-285-2221.

Implicit Bias Can Be Eliminated by Awareness

Being born in 1956, I grew up in the television age of the Western. In those days, all cowboys were white and male, their cooks were usually Chinese, and the only visual difference between the cowboys was the color of their hats and horses. Good cowboys wore white hats and rode white horses. The bad cowboys wore black hats and rode black horses. Fifty-five years later, has this affected how I deal with race in the courtroom? New research suggests that it has.

The bad news is that most of us are biased. Even worse, the bias is unconscious. The good news is that this type of bias can be eliminated through awareness, and the Section of Litigation is leading the way. "It is no exaggeration whatsoever to say that the research Professor Rachlinski and his colleagues are doing is probably the most important research about the justice system that is being conducted anywhere in the country today," said Judge Delissa A. Ridgway of the U.S. Court of International Trade as she kicked off the plenary session on implicit bias at a Leadership Meeting of the Section of Litigation. Ridgway was cochair of the Section's Task Force on Implicit Bias.

Professor Jeffrey J. Rachlinski of Cornell Law School took Section leaders through the current research on implicit bias. With the help of an electronic polling system, he instructed the leaders while they took a shortened version of the Implicit Association Test (IAT). The IAT is designed to uncover a variety of invidious associations such as white/good and black/bad or male/career and female/family. He followed this with an eyewitness test in which subjects generally tend to pick more "stereotypically African-American" suspects out of a street scene, using considerations like darker skin, when they were told the crime was one of violence versus a crime of fraud.

"The plan all along has been to put together a 'tool box' of information by which initially our Task Force, and then others, would be able to go out and make presentations," says Hilarie Bass, Miami, FL, past Chair of the Section. "If we do nothing more than make people realize that, even though they think they are completely unbiased and race- and gender-neutral, all of us are unconsciously affected by subliminal biases we do not even know exist. The best cure thus far for this implicit bias is awareness."

The Section has partnered with the National Center of State Courts to address implicit bias in the judicial system. The "tool box" includes such resources as how to administer the IAT, a video on the problem of implicit bias in the justice system, and a follow-up outline that can be tailored to specific jurisdictions.

"We wanted to get people the resources they need to present these issues to their firms, bar associations, or at judicial conferences," adds Bass.

U.S. District Judge Bernice B. Donald of the Western District of Tennessee, a Section Delegate to the ABA House of Delegates and member of its Committee on Issues of Concern to the Legal Profession, particularly focused on the need for detailed voir dire to probe these issues. She made the research come alive to the audience through a story from her courtroom about stereotyping.

"I remember selecting a jury once in a drug case," recalled Donald. "A public defender stepped up with her African-American defendant seated behind her at the table. She asked, 'How many of you know what a drug dealer looks like?' and the hands shot up. She didn't say anything else. Then, you could see the hands slowly go down as the people recognized what they were saying. The defendant sitting at the table looked like someone right out of central casting. If she had asked them to describe a 'drug dealer,' they would have described her client."

So, given the fact that we have been fed a steady diet of white/good and black/bad or female/family and male/career, what do you do when confronted with these issues? What if your client is black and everyone else in the courtroom is white? What if you're trying to get custody for a father and the judge is a woman?

Before I launch into this, I want tell you something about this particular column. When I reach the practical advice portion of this column, I send out a request to seasoned trial lawyers for their advice. I have never had a problem getting great responses to my questions. Last week I sent a request posing these issues to five trial attorneys. For the first time in over a decade, no one responded before my deadline.

Am I reading too much into this, or are issues of race and sex truly "the third rail" of trial work? Are people so concerned about being misunderstood in even addressing these issues that they prefer to ignore them altogether?

Here's the problem. You can hardly ask, "Your Honor, would you mind terribly asking the venire if they would take the IAT before jury selection?" Although it would be nice to know how well or poorly a potential juror, or the judge in a bench trial, might fare on the test, you simply cannot test them.

However, all of the research seems to indicate that once people are made aware of implicit bias, it disappears. So, how do you address the 800-pound gorilla in the room without making the 800-pound gorilla mad? People simply don't like it when others accuse them of being biased, even if on an unconscious level.

One technique would be to do what the public defender did in Judge Donald's courtroom. It certainly made the point crystal clear, but at the same time, there is the risk of embarrassing those potential jurors who raised their hands. Is there a step back from that technique?

From my perspective, here's the dynamic. You want to make the trier of fact aware that implicit bias may be a factor. You are worried that addressing it will be misinterpreted as, "Counsel, are you implying I'm a racist?"

The added dynamic for the other side is that once implicit bias is raised, the pendulum will swing too far in the other direction. You fear that the judge or jury will ignore the facts and ignore the law just to make the point that they are not racist or sexist.

A veteran prosecutor, who did not want to be quoted, told me that his experience with all-white juries and a minority defendant is that those juries tend to give the minority defendant the benefit of the doubt that they do not extend to a white defendant.

In most jurisdictions, judges begin with cautionary instructions that tell the potential jurors that they are not to consider a person's sex, race, religion, sexual orientation, or national ancestry in deciding the case. The problem is that you want to highlight your specific concern and not have it lumped in with everything else. One way would be to ask the judge to inquire on the specific concern, such as race. This avoids you having to do it.

If the judge declines to single out the factor of concern to you, you may opt for something gentle such as, "Ladies and gentlemen, as you can see, most of you are white, I'm white, the prosecutor's white, and the judge is white. Mr. Smith is black. Will you promise to follow the judge's instruction that a person's race is not a factor in this case?" If permitted, you could ask potential jurors if they have taken the IAT and what they thought of it, with the hope of educating the entire venire through that one juror.

You have opportunities in opening and closing. Perhaps in a bench trial in which you are seeking custody for the father, you might begin with, "Your Honor, although the 'tender years' doctrine of young children always being awarded to the mother has been overturned, it appears to be alive and well in a few cases. In this case, the father is seeking custody based on the following factors." Once again, a gentle reminder of bias, without a flat-out accusation of bias against this particular judge.

In closing, you could perhaps construct an argument based on the IAT such as, "Ladies and gentlemen, we are bombarded in society that black is bad and white is good. The bad cowboy always wore a black hat. We use phrases such as 'black magic.' Well, there is a reason that the figure of justice always wears a blindfold, and that is the race of a person simply does not, and should not, matter."

Resources:

Implicit Bias in the Judicial System (Section of Litigation website), *available* at www.americanbar.org/groups/litigation/initiatives/good_works/implicit_bias_in_the_judicial_system.html.

Jeffrey J. Rachlinski et al., "Does Unconscious Racial Bias Affect Trial Judges?", 84 *Notre Dame L. Rev.* 1195 (2009).

More details about the IAT are *available* at https://implicit.harvard.edu/implicit.

Don't Let the Judge Cut You Out

He peers over his bench, and you know what's coming. His head starts nodding up and down rhythmically, like one of those dogs in the back windows of some cars. You then hear these words, "Now Mrs. Jones, even though your father was a police officer, your three brothers are officers, and your husband is an officer, you can be a fair and impartial juror, can't you."

The juror looks down, then she says, "I can." You grit your teeth and burn another preemptory challenge.

Ask a trial judge the purpose of voir dire and the answer will be short. "In my opinion, the purpose of jury selection is to assure that the jury is fair and unbiased," says Hon. John G. Koeltl, New York City, member of the ABA Section of Litigation's Federal Practice Task Force. "It is not to use the process to slant the jurors to your side," he adds.

Ask a trial lawyer the purpose of voir dire and the answer will be different. "The lawyers are interested in a partial jury. I do not want an impartial jury. I want a jury that is in my favor from the beginning, and you can quote me on that," says Paul Mark Sandler, Baltimore, cochair of the Section of Litigation's Institute for Trial Training and chair of the Special Committee on Voir Dire for the Maryland State Bar Association. "I do believe that cases are won and lost with the selection of the jury," he opines.

The trial lawyer's answer to that question will also be longer. Entire books have been written on voir dire. Jury consultants put their children through college on voir dire.

So, I will assume you agree with Sandler that cases are won and lost in jury selection. But if you were to voir dire me, I would reveal two biases.

First, toward the end of my career as a trial attorney, I was espousing what I called, "I'll take the first 12 honest people not directly related to the other party theory." By this point in my career, I was no longer sure I could divine which way they were leaning by asking what magazines they subscribe to, what cars they drove, or noting the watch they wore into the courtroom. Second, I am a state court judge who always allows the attorneys to question, and I never try to rehabilitate a juror once an attorney has established a bias.

State or Federal Court?

So, if your participation in voir dire is so crucial to your case, do you have a choice of a court that will give you more voir dire? "There is a difference between jury trial procedures in federal and state courts as to whether to allow the attorneys to conduct voir dire," says Hon. Marvin E. Aspen, Chicago, United States District Court for the Northern District of Illinois and past cochair of the Section's Pretrial Practice and Discovery Committee. "There is a great variance of practice among the states, between counties within a state and even between individual state judges on the same court. The same is true in the federal system."

So, could you file in either state court or federal court? Wherever the case may be, could you file a motion for change of venue or judge?

You may have more control than you think. The usual mantra is that you get more attorney voir dire in state court. I have heard lawyers from Texas joke that you could almost try your entire case during voir dire if you were in state court in Texas. The mantra for federal court is that you don't get voir dire. Is that fact or fiction?

Voir Dire Atrophy in Federal Courts

"The general practice [in federal court] is that the judge conducts voir dire and usually asks the attorneys to submit, in writing, questions the attorneys may wish the judge to ask," says Judge Aspen, who was a state trial court judge for eight years before moving to the federal bench. "Somewhat of a hybrid method, which I have used, is for the judge to conduct voir dire and then also allow the attorneys a limited amount of time to ask supplementary questions," he continues. "However, since the art of attorney voir dire has atrophied so significantly in the federal system in recent years, I have found that most lawyers will now decline this offer."

Let's admit it: There are some questions you want the judge to ask. You would rather have the judge ask whether an individual juror or someone close to him has ever been involved in a court case, especially when a respected member of the community feels compelled to reveal that he got busted for pot three decades ago while in college. You don't want to be on the receiving end of that answer.

"My procedure is on our court's website," says Hon. Robert W. Gettleman, Chicago, United States District Court for the Northern District of Illinois. "I ask the questions in open court and then use the sidebar for follow-up questions with the attorneys. I think it may be a myth that attorneys are not involved in voir dire in federal court."

Ask for Voir Dire

Even if you hear through the grapevine that a particular judge does not let the attorneys ask questions, still ask for it. "One of my colleagues once told me that no lawyer had ever asked him to be given the opportunity to ask questions," says Judge Koeltl.

Trial attorney David Berg writes, "Trial lawyers in the Southern District of Texas argued for individual voir dire so consistently for such a long period of time that at least half the judges now allow it in some meaningful form."

"I have given attorneys voir dire in every case in addition to using a written questionnaire," says Hon. Barbara M. G. Lynn, Dallas, past Chair of the Section of Litigation and current national cochair of its Judicial Intern Opportunity Program. "The average time they ask for, and usually receive, is between 30 and 45 minutes."

If you ask for voir dire and are turned down, ask for a written questionnaire. People are more likely to be forthright with their views if allowed to respond to questions in writing on a sheet of paper, as opposed to being asked general questions en masse or being singled out and asked the question by a judge with scores of people listening. "Notwithstanding the presumption of innocence, we found many, many potential jurors who, in response to a written questionnaire, presumed the defendant to be guilty or he would not have been indicted," recalls Sandler.

Know the Law on Voir Dire

Know that cases, even in the federal system, have been reversed when the voir dire was not adequate. In *Fietzer v. Ford Motor Co.,* the court stated that a trial court ". . . should permit a reasonably extensive examination of prospective jurors so that the parties have a basis for an intelligent exercise of the right to challenge."

The key to using that standard is to note the words "reasonably extensive" and "parties." If you frame the issue as you versus the judge and who is better at doing an adequate voir dire, you are probably going to lose that battle. But you might make more headway if you reframe the discussion in terms of your client, his rights, and his desire to have you involved in the voir dire.

"I have convinced a judge who was dead set against us doing voir dire to give us some time," remembers Sandler. "His concern was that it would take too much time. I told the court that if he established the time, we could do it, and he agreed. It was very rewarding since the client felt that his lawyers were involved right from the beginning. If clients have a constitutional right to a jury trial, I believe they have a constitutional right to have their lawyer involved in voir dire."

Finally, read appellate court opinions to see how opportunities in voir dire have been wasted. In one case, counsel was allowed to question the jury for 30 minutes, which was 10 minutes longer than the usual. On appeal, he argued that this limitation prevented him from determining whether the all-white jury harbored biased racial attitudes. The appellate court noted that counsel did not ask any questions about race during his 30 minutes did not indicate what he would have asked if given additional time, and did not explain his failure to object or ask for additional time when the court indicated his time was up.

In another case, the court placed no time limit on voir dire provided the questions were kept within reason and relevance. After a time, the court told counsel that he had five additional minutes to ask germane or reasonable questions. In denying a motion for a new trial based, in part, on limiting counsel's voir dire, the court noted that a considerable amount of time had been spent on topics such as what football team any particular juror supported to whether he had heard the song "Que Sera Sera."

In some courts, voir dire is a gift. Use it wisely.

Resources:

Art Press, Ltd. v. Western Printing Machinery Company, 791 F.2d 616 (7th Cir. 1986).

Fietzer v. Ford Motor Co., 622 F.2d 281 (7th Cir. 1980).

U.S. v. Smallwood, 188 F.3d 905 (7th Cir. 1999).

Browne v. Signal Mountain Nursery, L.P., 286 F. Supp. 2d 904 (E.D. Tenn. 2003).

David Berg, *The Trial Lawyer: What It Takes to Win* (ABA Publ. 2006) *available at* http://shop.americanbar.org/eBus/Store/ProductDetails.aspx?productId=214881.

A Peer May Be Your Client's Worst Juror

Do You Want Your Peers Judging You?

When I first started trying cases, the selection of the jury was the part that made me the most nervous. I could plan for opening, direct, cross, and closing. With jury selection, I felt I was working without a net. So, I started reading everything I could find on the topic.

Some of the books and articles on jury selection from the 1950s were absolutely hilarious. One book—I have forgotten the title—advised that if you were doing insurance defense work, to pick Norwegians because they were conservative. So, I found myself in the cornfields of Illinois, looking for guys named Olaf to be on my jury.

From high school civics and on, we have heard the phrase "a jury of your peers." The phrase does not actually appear in the U.S. Constitution. The Magna Carta appears to be the source of the concept of being judged by your peers or equals. The concept back then, however, was that you would be judged by persons of your same social standing, status, or peerage as opposed to the crown.

As a young attorney, I took a rather simplistic approach. I wanted jurors who were like my client. After years of trying cases, my question now is: Do you really want a jury of your peers?

Anecdotal Experiences with Peers

Several anecdotes from real life bring the question into focus. Early in my career, I defended a young, female teenage driver. So, I picked as many young, female teenage drivers as I could find in the venire. I truly tried to get a jury of her peers.

On what I thought was an open-and-shut case, the jury was out for hours. Eventually, they found in our favor. When I interviewed the jurors who were willing to stick around, they told me that I had made a mistake by picking her peers. When I asked why, they said they were willing to give her the benefit of the doubt, but that her peers judged her much more harshly.

I usually tell this story in my one-day advocacy seminar. After I do, attorneys often come up to me and share their own "jury of peers" stories.

A prosecutor told me he was preparing to try his first case of sex with a minor. His supervisor asked his jury selection strategy. He told her that he was going to pick as many females who had daughters the same age as the victim.

His supervisor, who was a veteran of these cases, told him to pick as many men as he could find as close to age of the defendant. He was dumbfounded and asked "Why?" She said that the men will be disgusted by this guy, look down on him, and view themselves as the young victim's protectors. He won the case and was shocked when five of the male jurors showed up for the defendant's sentencing. This had never happened before.

On the defense side, a black public defender shared this story. She said when she started practicing, she tried to get as many blacks as possible on the jury if her defendant was black. She said she lost many cases.

So, she decided to switch her strategy and packed the jury with as many white jurors as possible. She started winning cases and hanging juries. She believed that the black jurors in her community judged the black defendant more harshly than the white jurors.

Resist the Urge to Stereotype

A jury of my peers would be a group of overweight, balding, white male judges. Would I really want a jury made up of people like me? Wouldn't they tend to judge me more harshly than perhaps persons different from me?

So why do we do it? Why do we stereotype people when in our hearts we know that human behavior is so complex? Why do we stereotype when we know that even if we had a day to question each juror, we could only touch the surface of their life experience?

"Do not overestimate the significance of demographics," says Theodore O. Prosise, Ph.D., Seattle, Tsongas Litigation Consulting, Inc. "Characteristics such as race, gender, or class can be useful, but they are extremely error-prone and can be highly misleading. The attractiveness of data that is easy to collect and stereotype is hard to overcome."

"Experiences and attitudes are far more important," continues Prosise. "A lot of times people look at the surface and judge poorly or misinterpret just because they are only looking at the demographics."

"My admonition is usually the juror you think you want is not the one you want, or the easy way to say it is that stereotypes never hold true," advises Anthony N. Upshaw, Miami, past codirector of the Section's Division IV—Procedural. "For example, I may be defending and the plaintiff may be a well-off, Caucasian female bringing a wrongful death action for the death of her husband.

"On first impression, you might think that you wouldn't want jurors that are also well-off, older, white females," Upshaw continues. "Yet they may feel entirely different due to their own life experiences. Knowing their beliefs on a topic is much more important than any stereotype or superficial evaluation of a particular juror," he concludes.

Be Wary of Putting "Experts" on the Jury

"We take the approach of jury de-selection or eliminating those people that, because of bias or prejudice, are going to be potentially more critical of a party than they should be," advises Prosise. "When we are on the defense side of an employment case, one of the highest risk jurors are ones with HR (human resources) experience. While they may be a peer of the person who made the decision for the defendant, you risk having them become a non-testifying expert in the jury room where the rest of the jury looks to them as an opinion leader."

So, do you really want a doctor or a nurse on the jury in a medical malpractice case? Do you really want an accountant on the jury in an accounting malpractice case? If you are defending, that juror may be your client's peer but may also be your client's worst nightmare in the jury room. They may bring in their own life experiences, advice, and standards, and apply them to your client.

"Another concern is where a juror may contradict the law as the judge would give it, based upon their personal experience," cautions Prosise. "In construction defect cases where we would be representing the general contractor, the legal instruction is that the general has a right to rely on the expertise of the subcontractor. We've had plenty of instances in mock trials with a subcontractor on the jury who says, 'Oh that's not the case at all. The general contractor is responsible for anything, and if I make a mistake, it is their fault.'"

In terms of strategy, it seems clear from our experts on the topic that attitudes and experiences clearly trump basic demographics. Simply stated, I guess we have arrived at the old saying "You can't judge a book by its cover."

How to Remove the Juror Gracefully

So let's say that you are able to probe attitudes and experiences. You find out that a potential juror who, on the surface, looks like a peer of your client, is not good for you. You don't want him or her on your jury. What message do you send to the rest of the venire when you kick the nurse off a medical malpractice case or an ironworker off a construction case? How do you avoid sending a message that you don't want people who may know the most about the topic on the jury?

Well, if you have to exercise your challenges in front of the entire venire, you are kind of stuck. You can try to question whether they can set their experiences in the field aside and base their decision on the evidence presented so as to sensitize the entire panel and them of your concern. Then, if they try to dominate the deliberations, the other 11 jurors will remind that juror of his promise to you to leave his experiences at the door and base the verdict only on the evidence at trial.

A better approach is to have the judge excuse the juror. All challenges are made outside the presence of the venire. If this procedure is agreed to at the start, neither side is disadvantaged. The venire does not know who excused which potential juror or for what reason, thus eliminating one aspect of gamesmanship for both sides. As anecdotally noted above, both sides may have very good reasons why their clients' peers would not be the best judges of them.

How About a Free Shadow Jury?

Inside the Juror's Mind

How would you like to know what the jury is thinking? How would you like a shadow jury without having to pay for one? What if this shadow jury were your real jurors?

"It is like having a free shadow jury out in the audience because you could tell what was happening going through the trial," said Russell "Rusty" Hardin Jr., Houston, a member of the ABA Section of Litigation's Trial Attorney Advisory Board during a panel discussion entitled "Baseball, A Governor & Successful Trial Strategies in High Profile Cases," presented in September 2012, at the Section's fall leadership meeting in St. Louis. Hardin, who secured an acquittal on all charges for Roger Clemens, and Sam Adam Jr., Chicago, who defended Illinois Governor Rod Blagojevich in his first trial, were panelists on the program moderated by Hilarie Bass, Miami, past chair of the Section.

"Allowing jurors to submit written questions during the evidence phase of the trial gives the lawyers and the judge a window into the juror's thinking," agrees Hon. James F. Holderman, Chicago, cochair of the Section's Special Committee on Jury Innovations. "It allows the lawyers and judges to dispel any misconceptions the jurors otherwise may have."

In 2004, then ABA President Robert Grey established the American Jury Project, which was chaired by former chair of the Section, Patricia Lee Refo, Phoenix. One of the innovations was to allow jurors to submit questions, to be asked by the judge, after sorting out any objections or modifications from counsel.

Mandating Jury Questions

Several states, such as Indiana, Colorado, and Arizona, have mandated that courts allow jury questions for all jury trials. Effective July 1, 2012, the Illinois Supreme Court implemented a new rule allowing juror questions—but for only civil cases. States vary widely on procedures in this area. One such area is whether the judge or counsel asks the questions and when they ask the questions. Counsel should check with the trial judge on how he or she handles questions in the courtroom.

"I was opposed to it originally. I had reservations, but I loved it," said Hardin. "The judge in our case did not allow recross. The government was putting on their case. It was direct, cross, redirect then, 'No, Mr. Hardin, nothing further, stop. Any of the jurors have any questions?'"

When the primary agent in the Clemens trial testified, the jurors had 29 questions for him. "One of the questions was 'Do you think you have perhaps overstepped in this case?'" reports Hardin. "That question was not asked, but it sure was nice to know. When the government put their physical evidence in, there were 32 questions . . . and they were very, very good questions. They were most attentive."

"The jurors appreciate the opportunity to inquire, are more engaged and attentive to the evidence presented by the lawyers," confirms Judge Holderman. As authority for the concept's use in the Seventh Circuit, the project manual gives this succinct quote on the benefits of jury questions from *United States v. Sutton*, "Juror-inspired questions may serve to advance the truth by alleviating uncertainties in the jurors' minds, clearing up confusion, or alerting the attorneys to points that bear further elaboration. Further, it is at least arguable that a question-asking juror will be a more attentive juror."

Hardin told the audience that his favorite question which, again, was not asked, was for the main accuser. It was "In light of all the lies you've told, why should we believe you?" Questions like these, although not asked, give counsel the inside track on what is going on in at least one juror's mind. This insight can help with trial strategy, questioning of other witnesses, and thoughts for closing argument.

"She [the clerk] would take the questions to the bench," continued Hardin. "We would approach the bench, he [the judge] would put on the white noise, the jurors couldn't hear and he would read the questions, we would object or not object and he would read the [approved] questions."

"My experience in the seven-month test was that most of the jurors' questions sought information to clarify evidence that had been presented during the lawyers' questioning of the witness," says Judge Holderman. "Rarely did the jurors' questions seek testimony on a subject that was inadmissible, and when such questions were submitted, I explained to the jury why the question could not be asked."

Procedures Used

The procedure under most systems is for the court to make the questions part of the record and disclose the questions to the parties outside the hearing of the jury. Counsel may then interpose objections or suggest modifications to the question. The court may then decide when the question should be asked, and whether counsel should ask the question or the court should ask the question.

The Seventh Circuit's manual includes a preliminary instruction to the jury, advising them of their right to ask questions, that the judge will determine whether a question should be asked or asked in a modified form, and that they are to make no inferences if a question is not asked and not put any greater weight to a question that was asked. Likewise, there is a suggested jury instruction for use at the end of the trial.

Most states that use this procedure give the courts flexibility. The Committee Comments to Illinois Supreme Court Rule 243 state, in part, "The trial judge may discuss with the parties' attorneys whether the procedure will be helpful in the case, but the decision whether to use the procedure rests entirely with the trial judge. The rule specifies some of the procedures the trial judge must follow, but it leaves other details to the trial judge's discretion." Critics of the system raise issues such as delay of the trial process, whether the system favors less-competent lawyers, promotes premature deliberations, promotes more questions during deliberations, or causes jurors to try to shape the evidence one way or the other.

"I would recommend this procedure to all of you," counters Hardin. "The jury would write out their questions . . . and, believe it or not, this did not take long at all. It really did not stretch this trial out."

"My procedure was to instruct the jurors that if they had a question, they should write it down and then raise a hand, holding the folded paper aloft," says Judge Holderman. "My clerk then would unobtrusively retrieve, photocopy, and distribute the jurors' questions to counsel while witness testimony proceeded, took no time away from the testimony."

"I did not observe jurors filling in evidentiary gaps for lawyers, premature deliberations, nor more questions during deliberations; if anything, I had fewer," says Judge Holderman. "I saw no juror become an advocate, shift the burden of proof, or try to shape the evidence one way or the other through juror questions. The jurors I observed during the test period acted with the same conscientious resolve to do the right thing that I observed throughout my career in the legal profession."

Historical Perspective

Perhaps the reluctance to involve jurors in the questioning is one of the last vestiges of the original jury system of hundreds of years ago. Then it was a system that primarily decided issues regarding property and inheritances, and the jurors selected were those from the community who knew the most about the subject. We now have come full circle and want jurors who do not know anything about the subject matter or the people involved. If they do, they are challenged for cause.

Given that we are usually dealing with blank slates when it comes to our jurors, doesn't it just make sense that we make sure that the most important people in the court, other than the parties, have their questions answered? Given the safeguards utilized in most courts coupled with our opportunity to modify the questions posed, don't we want jurors who are attentive and listening, and might have a question?

An ancient Chinese proverb says, "Tell me and I'll forget; show me and I may remember; involve me and I'll understand." Is there any downside to your jurors getting more involved in your case? Trial lawyers are always looking for ways to keep the jurors' attention when it is four o'clock in the afternoon, the sun is streaming in, the courtroom is warm, and an accountant is on the stand. Maybe if jurors know they have a chance to question or clarify, they just may stay awake.

Resources:

"Baseball, A Governor & Successful Trial Strategies in High Profile Cases," *available at* www.americanbar.org/groups/litigation/events_cle/live-streaming.html.

Hon. James F. Holderman, "Trying the ABA's Principles for Juries and Jury Trials," *Litigation*, Volume 33, Number 3, Spring 2007. The author thanks Judge Holderman for allowing him to quote liberally from this more detailed article on this subject.

Seventh Circuit Jury Project Manual, *available at* www.7thcircuitbar.org/associations/1507/files/01ProjectManual.pdf.

"Principles for Juries and Jury Trials," *available at* http://bit.ly/LN382-principles.

United States v. Sutton, 970 F. 2d 1001, 1005 n.3 (1st Cir. 1992).

CHAPTER 3

TRIAL PRESENTATION

Brain Science for the Courtroom: Tips for Attention and Retention

It weighs, on the average, three pounds. It is nearly 80 percent water, and if the neurons were laid end to end, they would stretch almost to the moon. It is, of course, what decides our cases—the human brain. International education consultant David A. Sousa, Ed.D., condenses years of brain research in his book, *How Brain Science Can Make You a Better Lawyer.* Dr. Sousa is the author of seven best-selling books on how to turn brain research into strategies for improving learning.

Sousa practices what he preaches. Less is more and shorter is better. The book is 182 pages, divided into four chapters. Each chapter is divided into tips backed by brain research. Included is an appendix on basic brain facts, a glossary to define terms, and suggested reference material for those who want to dig deeper.

The book starts with five tips on understanding the human brain in general and seven tips on your brain in the workplace, but the bulk of the book is the 19 tips on brain science as applied to practice. Many of the concepts confirm what experienced trial lawyers have done instinctively throughout their practice.

Sousa first explores the concept that we humans learn and retain information from the brain stem up. The brain stem is the survival center. It learns and retains information fast, as when a child quickly learns—and never forgets— that the stove is hot. The brain stem must be satisfied first before the higher areas of the brain come into play.

When I train attorneys in trial work, I try to make them remember this brain point by my gross exaggeration, "You cannot learn your multiplication tables while drowning." That is why the jurors' physical surrounding is so important. If they are too hot, too cold, can't see, or can't hear, learning and retention are blocked. The brain stem is so occupied with issues of hot and cold that the higher areas of the brain do not engage.

"If I think it is a little warm or if they cannot see due to lighting, I will ask the court to check with them to see what they need," says Jeffrey Kroll, Chicago, former Section of Litigation Council member. "I want to be the guide, the person the jurors are following, and as much as possible, without crossing the line, I want to be one of them. It is a fine line, and you don't want to appear to be condescending," Kroll suggests.

Sousa's book then moves to the part of the brain that sits right over the brain stem. This is the emotional center. Sousa tells us that emotional experiences are also processed quickly and stored permanently. In addition, Sousa reminds us that how a person feels about a learning experience determines the attention he or she will devote to that experience.

We must always remember that the day before our trial, our jurors were mowing lawns, cooking dinners, paying bills. We have asked them, actually forced them, to leave the comfort of their homes, to sit with people they don't know, and to answer questions about their personal lives in front of strangers. Many come into court with the emotional state of apprehension, perhaps even fear, and certainly with a feeling of intrusion on their time. The great trial attorneys are very aware of this dynamic and do not take this lightly. They are able to show genuine concern and appreciation for the jurors without being overly solicitous.

Once the trial attorney satisfies the jurors' emotional needs, he or she can then try to get the jurors involved in the client's case on an emotional level. If the trial attorney can engage the juror's brain on both the reasoning level and the emotional level, he or she has gone a long way to getting a favorable verdict for the client.

Turning to tips for presenting factual information, Sousa's Tip 3:10 deals with the crucial concepts of primacy and recency. Whether it be opening, direct, cross, or closing, we tend to remember what happened first and what happened last.

"When it comes to direct, in terms of primacy, I like to use headlines at the very front of the exam to alert the jurors as to why this person is being called in this case," counsels Kroll. "I may ask the doctor a headline question to frame his or her opinion especially if it is at the beginning of what may be an hour and a half direct examination."

To illustrate primacy and recency, Sousa includes a graph showing the degree of retention across a 20-minute learning episode in addition to a chart showing degree of attention related to the time of day. Knowing these principles helps structure the order of your witnesses. "If I have an important fact witness or medical doctor, I want those witnesses on first," advises Kroll. "I may bury my boring accounting witness right after lunch because I just need the numbers out there for my close," he says.

"If my expert has been pummeled in a videotape deposition, I will try to put that on right after lunch. I have no hesitancy in putting a less-than-favorable witness on later in the morning or right after lunch when the jury is starting to get tired," Kroll says.

These same principles apply to you as well as your witnesses. If you are going to make a mistake, it will most likely be at the end of the day. "I tried a case with a very experienced attorney on the other side," recalls Kroll. "I noticed that he yawned a lot and became visibly tired in the afternoon, so I changed the order of my witnesses and put my medical expert on late in the day. His cross of my expert was less effective than the crosses I had seen him do earlier in the morning."

Sousa explores methods to gain the advantage and perhaps, more importantly, what to do when you are at a disadvantage.

For example, what if you don't have the advantage of primacy or recency when it comes to closing argument? He gives concrete suggestions of how to overcome having to close as the defense when the plaintiff gets to go both first and last.

Sousa explains the differences between visual, auditory, and kinesthetic learners. People tend to lean toward one method of processing information, whether it be with their eyes, their ears, or simply their gut. He gives tips on dealing with concepts both verbally and visually, while appealing to all three different types of learners. He includes tests you can take to find out if you are more of a left brain (logical and analytical) or right brain (intuitive and visual) thinker.

"People do learn and comprehend things differently," notes Kroll. "Some lawyers are too afraid of the 'asked and answered' objection. I will ask the witness a question, I will then show the witness an exhibit to communicate the point both verbally and visually, and I don't think that is being cumulative. We, as lawyers, need to mix it up a bit to keep their attention, whether it is showing them a visual, changing your position in the courtroom, or using vocal inflection."

In light of the flood of televised courtroom dramas, the concepts of both positive and negative transfer are discussed in Sousa's book. Each juror has prior knowledge and experiences that they bring to the table. The transfer of their life experience onto the palette of your case may be good or may be bad.

One example Sousa addresses is how television can transfer into the courtroom, especially with regard to the burden of proof. Some of the more popular shows are *CSI* and *Law and Order* and all of their variations. So, after watching these shows, what is the burden of proof in the mind of the typical juror? It is probably beyond a reasonable doubt. Do you need to address this possible negative transfer if you are the plaintiff in a civil case? You certainly should. Preponderance of the evidence is not discussed much on these shows.

If you are a prosecutor in a criminal case, what type of evidence does the jury expect after watching these shows? They have been bombarded with episodes where there is always a fingerprint, always a blood, tissue, or hair sample, all of which are tested in a lab that looks like the inside of NASA.

Sousa's book is packed with hands-on tests such as one on memory retention linked to the number of points made. He gives concrete examples on simplifying language and creating visuals that work. Decades of brain research have been distilled for the trial lawyer's use in court.

Resource:

David A. Sousa, Ed. D., *How Brain Science Can Make You a Better Lawyer* (ABA 2009), available from the ABA Web Store at www.ababooks.org or call (800) 285-2221.

Handling the Bad Stuff in Court

He removed the wrong disc. The patient had an extra set of ribs. The surgeon miscounted and removed the wrong disc. The verdict? Zero.

Back in the 1990s, I defended a doctor who assisted the primary surgeon in removing a compromised disc. The plaintiff kept my doctor in the case long enough to get his testimony at trial and then dismissed the claim against him. I asked my co-counsel if he intended to admit liability and try it on damages. He said, "No." I asked, somewhat incredulously, "What's the defense?" His response: "S--t happens."

I kept in touch with the circuit clerk and followed the case. Several mornings later I called, and the conversation went something like this:

> Me: "Have they come back?"
> Clerk: "Yes."
> Me: "What they'd give her?"
> Clerk: "Nothing."
> Me: "What?"
> Clerk: "Nothing, no liability."
> Me: "Why?"
> Clerk: "They didn't like her; they really liked him."

The conversation went on, and the clerk explained that the plaintiff came off as overreaching and not likeable. The doctor was a (I am going to date myself here) Marcus Welby sort: likeable, down-to-earth, and well-respected in the community. She had an extra set of ribs. He miscounted. They gave him a pass.

The criminal defense bar faces this every day. They have clients who are not particularly likeable or have done something odious. But what of the civil case? What can we learn from our colleagues on the criminal side?

On the civil side, most of us can choose, or not choose, to represent a particular client. First, I will assume that you believe in your client and your client's position. If you do not, someone else should try the case. With that said, we begin.

The first step is how you relate to your client in front of potential jurors. Please remember that potential jurors are walking on the same sidewalk and riding in the same elevator with you and your client on the first day of jury selection. I cannot tell you the number of times I have seen counsel talk and treat clients in a different manner outside the courtroom, thinking no one is listening. Once seated in the courtroom, the potential jurors have nothing to do except watch and evaluate how you relate to them, the judge, opposing counsel, and, especially, your client.

"Any great trial lawyer will tell you, there are no set rules for trial," says James J. Brosnahan, San Francisco, legendary trial lawyer, instructor for the Section of Litigation's Litigation Institute for Trial Training and past recipient of the ABA Pro Bono Publico Award. "As a young lawyer I watched the real courtroom warhorses and learned from them. You always stand by your client when the venire comes in, you chat with him or her, and you make it clear by use of voice, content, intonation, and gesture that you really care about this person," Brosnahan says.

One need only refer to the research done by Dr. Albert Mehrabian to know that the intonation we use, and the visual cues we give off, trump the actual words we say.

"A jury of people can tell how you feel about your client by watching how you present yourself before them with your words and your body language," echoes Paul Mark Sandler, Baltimore, chair of the Section's Special Committee on the Litigation Institute for Trial Training. "You don't want to be perceived as doing something contrived or insincere, but there may be a time when it would be appropriate to put my arm around him or her depending on the situation."

"In the final argument in the case against Steven Psinakis I stood behind him, put a hand on each shoulder, and said, 'It is time for Steven Psinakis to go home to the Philippines,'" recalls Brosnahan. Steven Psinakis did go home. He was acquitted.

"The key to humanizing the client is to understand your audience," says Sandler, as he turns to jury selection. "You want to approach it based upon what you think would resonate with your listener." And with jury selection, you have some say in who will be your listeners.

"In the John Walker Lindh case we decided that, if it went to trial, we wanted parents of children at least 12 years of age," says Brosnahan. "We wanted jurors that knew young people did things that are spontaneous; they are not evil, they just do things that teenage kids do.

"I have a general rule that the jurors that are going to hurt you the most are the ones that are most threatened by the alleged activity," continues Brosnahan. "I'm going to try a fraud case down in Los Angeles at the end of the month, and if somebody thinks they can be defrauded, they can be sensitive to that and maybe identify with the plaintiffs. The psychology of jury selection is something that nobody can spend too much time on."

Whether a jury likes or dislikes your client generally hinges on either who they are or what they have done. In general, who they are should be irrelevant, and the judge will help you by giving an instruction to that effect. However, what your client did or did not do is usually relevant.

For example, let's say my defendant driver, after the accident, went over and said something vile to the other driver. You file a motion in limine saying the prejudicial effect outweighs the probative value. You lose. The judge says, in effect, if your client is stupid enough to say those words, he's going to have to live with them at trial. The sole issue in the case is who had the duty to yield. You're afraid his words may trump any yield sign.

"There was a guy I worked construction with years ago, and I used to count to see if he could have a sentence that did not have the 'F' word in it," laughs Brosnahan. "That construction worker is not going to be too upset by language. The audience is everything."

"There is always bad stuff," says Brosnahan. "In courts where questioning is allowed, you get it out there early and gauge a potential juror's reaction. You must prepare them that they are going to hear this stuff. If you cannot do it in jury selection, you do it in your opening statement," he says.

In your examination of your client, where do you put the bad stuff? "Again, this is entirely situational," begins Brosnahan. "I don't think juries are too patient with the 'Did you help the Boy Scouts?' You can do some warm-up on background, but you may want to just start with, 'You are accused of tax fraud; did you cheat on your taxes?' I guess I would put the bad stuff somewhere in the middle, after you have done some background and had them explain what was going on and why. I don't think you want to put it at the end and set-up, or tee-up, the other side."

In the course of the trial, how do you address the bad stuff? "I was trying a case in Northern California when I asked my client why he did something," recalls Brosnahan. "His response was that God told him to do it. This was about 11:15 in the morning. I said to the judge that this would be a good time to take the lunch recess and, fortunately, he agreed."

"It was final argument," continues Brosnahan. "With my client sitting there, I said, 'Look, my client is very, very, strange; there are people like that in the world, but he is not a criminal.' In the hallway after the verdict, several jurors echoed my comment back to me and agreed he was strange, but not a criminal."

If there is an elephant in the courtroom, you have to acknowledge it. You maintain your credibility with the jury when you directly confront the warts on your case or client, separate for the jury what is truly relevant, argue the other side is throwing dirt for dirt's sake, and move on to what really is at issue.

"You admit to the jury as much as you can, and in that way, you keep your credibility and you keep their trust," counsels Brosnahan. "You frame the real issue for them. They are very smart and will say, 'Well, he admitted this and he admitted this other thing, but there is no question that the issue, as he put it, is what we really need to decide.'"

"Every case we try is our most important case," concludes Sandler. "We feel that we are the client and we are fighting hard. In one case, the judge was sentencing my client and telling me that he did not appreciate this particular crime and acted as if I was the one being sentenced. I had to remind the judge that I was going home to dinner. Of course, he caught on and agreed. That is what I mean by personal advocacy."

Resources:

Mark Curriden, "7 over 70, Lions of the Trial Bar," *ABA J.*, Mar. 1, 2009, *available at* www.abajournal.com.

Dan Morain, "Philippine Revolution Hero Acquitted in Explosives Case," *L.A. Times*, June 8, 1989.

Albert Mehrabian, Ph.D., www.kaaj.com/psych

Acting in Court: If All the World's a Stage, What's Court?

All the world's a stage
And all the men and women merely players
They have their exits and their entrances
And one man in his time plays many parts
—William Shakespeare, *As You Like It*, Act 2, Scene 7

This above all: to thine own self be true
And it must follow, as the night the day
Thou canst not then be false to any man
—William Shakespeare, *Hamlet*, Act 1, Scene 3

It was several years ago when I had some time to kill in a mall. I wandered into one of those pop-up calendar kiosks and thumbed through a quote of-the-day desk calendar for parents raising teens. For some reason, I remember this quote: "Teenage boys try on many faces, trying to find the face that fits them best." What faces have you tried on in court? Have they all worked?

At a recent trial training program, I critiqued a talented and articulate young advocate. I won't tell you her real name, but knowing she had a sense of humor, I told her that I could tell whether we were going to get "Good Betty" or "Bad Betty" simply based on whether it was a direct or cross. She adopted two completely different personas, one for each of those two tasks. Everything about her changed—her tone, her pace, her movement, and her facial expression. It was a real Jekyll and Hyde performance.

So which Shakespeare quote works best for the advocate in court? Is it best to try on different masks or to just be true to yourself—or is there something in between?

It Is OK to Vary the Pace

David Berg, in his must-read book for every trial lawyer, tells this story on himself, "Early on, I cross-examined everyone like they were axe murderers, including school teachers and old ladies: 'Exactly what do you mean, you were tending your roses?' and, 'Quit fiddling with your oxygen tank.'"

I once told a young attorney that he could not treat every witness on the other side of the case as if divine providence placed that person on this earth for the sole purpose of messing with his case. He would go after an 80-year-old occurrence witness to a traffic accident with a vengeance and a hostility that should perhaps be reserved only for the cross of an admitted pedophile.

Remember, chances are good that not everyone on your side is a saint—nor is everyone on the other side a sinner. At the risk of barding you with a bunch of Shakespeare, I bet he would advise you to "Fit the cross to the witness, the witness to the cross."

"Be yourself—your most prepared, professional, sincere and respectful self," advises Christina Plum, Milwaukee, cochair of the ABA Section of Litigation's Roundtables and member of its Continuing Education Committee. "I encourage the students [in my law school oral communications course] to work with their natural speaking styles and personalities. That doesn't prohibit them from changing their speaking styles, but they must remain true to how they communicate generally, to avoid being perceived as actors rather than advocates."

In my experience, both before and after moving to the bench, most young advocates leave their personality at the courthouse door. They are simply not themselves in court. They are bright, engaging people during the coffee break, but when they walk into the courtroom, everything changes. How they walk changes, how they talk changes.

Speak Plainly and Directly

"Before and after" becomes "prior and subsequent." No one ever "gets out of a car," they "exit a vehicle." No one ever "knows" or "sees" anything in court, they are "aware of" or "observe" things. I tell young attorneys that the test of what words they use in front of a jury, or a judge for that matter, is whether they use the words in real life.

In real life, you never say "I submit to you the toast is burnt." or "Dear, are we going to the movie prior or subsequent to dinner?" You can go your entire legal career never once saying "prior" or "subsequent" and you would be no less professional. I have never heard two jurors complaining, "Did you hear that in there, 'before and after'! What ever happened to 'prior and subsequent'?"

Test this theory. We live in an era of courtroom drama on television—and that is what the jurors are watching. Take an hour to watch one of those shows. I expect you won't hear a lot of "priors and subsequents" being thrown around.

For most young advocates, their biggest problem is that they feel they need to "act" like a lawyer. This usually means the adoption of a stilted way of communicating so that everyone within earshot knows he or she is in the presence of a person who went to law school.

Maintain a Consistent and Sincere Persona

A second persona problem is the shifting, inconsistent persona.

There are attorneys who are blissfully unaware that the other people riding the elevator with them may be jurors. I cannot count the number of times that I have overheard counsel, outside the courtroom, say something akin to, "Great chip in on 17 Reggie, see you at the club on Thursday?" only to then go into court and exclaim, "I am outraged by counsel!"

"People can see if you are sincere, and false sincerity does no good," counsels Paul Mark Sandler, Baltimore, cochair of the Section of Litigation's Litigation Institute for Trial Training. "A jury can tell how you feel about your client and your case. Your words, your body language must convey the sincerity and the purpose of your case. I try to convey that this is our most important case, we feel for and are fighting hard for our client."

I have been in a few plays for our local community theater, and people often remarked what a great combination that was—an actor and a trial lawyer. I usually responded that I really had to watch myself, for if the jury ever perceived I was acting, that was, by definition, false.

When have you been the most persuasive in your life? My guess is that it was an emotional event where you had a lot at stake—asking someone on a first date, defending yourself from a false accusation, or persuading a child to take another path. I tell young attorneys they probably have a wider range in real life than what they display in the courtroom. I then tell them they must take those same tools they used when persuading someone outside the courtroom and bring it inside the courtroom.

"That is what I mean by personal advocacy," agrees Sandler. "In one sentencing it went a little too far when the judge told me that he did not appreciate this particular crime and acted as if I was the one being sentenced. I had to remind the judge I was going home to dinner and it was the client being sentenced. Of course, he caught on right away and readily agreed."

Studies on communication tell us that most of the meaning in the English language comes from inflection and visual cues, as opposed to the actual words. The phrase "I love you" is almost totally dependent upon how it is said. Jurors and judges can quickly tell if you truly believe in your client and your case.

When I speak to civic groups, I am usually asked how an attorney can represent someone he or she knows is guilty. My response always is that, although attorneys may not believe their client, they do believe in our court system and their role in that system. They can do their job because they truly believe that their job is to put the prosecution to their burden of proving every element beyond a reasonable doubt; thus, they believe in their case and their obligation, whether or not they actually believe their client.

Deal with "Personality Plus"

At the far end of the bell curve are those attorneys who have personality plus and may need to dial it back a bit until the jury knows them better.

This applies only to a very small percentage of attorneys. Most attorneys have the opposite problem.

A close friend of mine who, by his verdicts and the judgment of his peers, is one of the most successful trial attorneys to be found, is one of those rare people who are just brimming with personality. When he advises younger attorneys cut from the same cloth, he tells them that early in his career, he lost a lot of cases because he had not learned to give the jury some time to get to know him.

In short, it appears that the wisdom from both *Hamlet* and *As You Like It* apply. We must be true to ourselves, or we come across as mere actors.

Real life, of course, gives us many roles—spouse, parent, friend, counselor, teacher—and in these roles we become very good at arguing for our own cause. Our clients deserve no less. Our clients deserve the same passion we tend to reserve for ourselves. The true advocate knows this.

Resources:

David Berg, "The Trial Lawyer: What It Takes to Win" (ABA Publ. 2006), *available at* http://tinyurl.com/LNw12-Berg.

If you would like to cure yourself of jargon forever, read footnote 1 in *U.S. v. Marshall*, 488 F.2d 1169 (9th Cir. 1973).

Lessons from a Luddite: Top 10 Tips for Visuals

"Hey Dad, can we have your phone?" The kids would take my phone to where their friends were gathered. I would then hear, "Hey, look!" and the room would dissolve in squeals of laughter.

My phone is light years behind their phones and so is my technological savvy. I am a Luddite. So, if I am able to make visual presentations, trust me, so can you.

Study after study tells us that the retention rate with information we both see and hear is between 70 and 80 percent. With just ears, it is between 10 and 15 percent.

Also, as the jury population ages, we are dealing with younger jurors who prefer their information to be visual and want their information fast. So, for those of you who have never tried it, here are my top 10 suggestions for getting started.

1. Steal It

If you see a presentation you like, ask the presenter to send it to you. Tell her that you are not going to steal her presentation, but you really like her set up, her fonts, her transition between slides, etc. and that you would like to use it as a template.

You can go on the Internet and find presentations to download. You then simply take your cursor, highlight the words or images you want to get rid of, and delete them. Then type in your own stuff or replace the images with whatever you want to use. It will appear in the font and color you like and will appear on the screen in the same way as the old presentation. Under "Resources," I have prepared a presentation showing different types of slides that you are welcome to steal.

2. Start Small

In each case, time overlays all the facts and all the witnesses. I found I could not adequately prepare a case until I created a visual chronology.

Only when you see the facts and witnesses in relation to time do things come clearly into focus. Was the day on which the witness claimed something happened a Saturday, a Sunday, a birthday, or an anniversary? Would that really have happened in the week between Christmas and New Year's?

The benefit of building a chronology is twofold. First, for your opening statement, having the date and the event associated with it helps the jury or judge retain that information. Second, the slides become your notes. They release you from reading an opening statement from a legal pad.

Lists are useful for cases with many witnesses. You can give the judge or jury the "cast of characters" for each side. The attorney whom the jury perceives as the person who is attempting to make the case understandable has the advantage.

3. Familiarize Yourself with the "Undo" Button

I was once asked what software I used to build presentations. I answered, and then someone asked whether I owned stock in that company. No, I do not own any stock in any computer company. I just happen to have Microsoft's presentation software, PowerPoint, loaded onto my computer.

In PowerPoint, the most useful feature I have found, since I make a lot of mistakes, is the "undo typing" button—the little button with the arrow that runs counterclockwise that will undo any mistake I make. I can keep on clicking it until I get back to the version I liked.

4. Ask a Teenager

If you're really stumped, ask a teenager. I was once trying to insert a graphic into a presentation and simply couldn't get it done. One of my children, who was about 10 at the time, came into the room and asked, "Dad, why are you talking to yourself?" Luckily, he had not heard what I was saying.

I explained to him what I was trying to do, and he asked to try. I thought to myself, "Good luck," and went into my favorite room to console myself—the kitchen. As I walked back, he was walking out and with an impish grin said, "Got it." Ask a teenager.

However, most teenagers pride themselves on doing this stuff so fast you cannot follow it. Bribe them to slow down so you can follow.

5. Remember That Your Screen Is Not the Courtroom

"See how the presentation will look in a courtroom where the jury is not two feet from a computer screen, but 20 feet away from an elevated screen," advises Harout J. Samra, Miami, FL, cochair of the ABA Section of Litigation's Technology for the Litigator Committee. "In that context, the color may not turn out exactly the same, and the size of text may not be exactly the same."

What may look great on your computer may not look great in a courtroom. Whatever you assemble, you need to take it to the room where it will be used, on the projector that will be used, against the screen or wall that will be used.

Most of my failures happened when I became too cute with colors. What appeared vivid and beautiful on my screen was washed out in the courtroom. I now use almost exclusively white letters on a black background or, if the room is particularly dark, black letters on a white background.

Finally, do not put too much information on each slide. Test to make sure you can read the letters from the last row at the far corner of the jury box.

6. Back Up Your Work

As you make your masterpiece, hit "save" often. I save it on my hard drive, copy it to a thumb drive, and then burn a CD. You will thank yourself for taking this belt, suspenders, and Velcro approach.

When it comes to actually using your presentation in the courtroom, I would also print out each slide. Any office supply store carries transparencies that will make overheads of your slides using a regular copier.

In our courtrooms, we have an LCD projector, an ELMO, and an old overhead projector. If the LCD went down, I could use the ELMO. If the ELMO's bulb burned out, I could use the overhead projector. If all three bulbs burned out at the same time, I would ask for a break.

For those of you who are inclined to stop reading at this point, I never had one bulb burn out, let alone three. Just knowing I had back-ups made me calmer.

7. Use Ctrl+c and Ctrl+v

Now we are really getting fancy. If you have a document—perhaps the emergency room report, a picture, or a statement that is in PDF form—you can highlight any of that document and copy the highlighted portion into your presentation.

On my computer, I have Adobe Acrobat, which allows me to click on any document and, with the left mouse button depressed, drag it and create a box which, when I let go of the button, the boxed portion of the document appears highlighted. I then hit "Ctrl+c," go to my PowerPoint, click on the slide where I want the excerpt to appear, hit "Ctrl+v," and the excerpt appears where I want it in the presentation. I can then click on it and move it, or click on any one of the corners, drag it, and make it larger. I simply repeat this technique to embed multiple objects into the presentation.

8. The "B" and "W" Keys Are Used to Highlight Visuals

Since most people prefer receiving information through their eyes, as opposed to their ears, you must turn off the visuals unless you are using them with the witness. The visual will always override the verbal.

In PowerPoint, press "B" on your keyboard, and your screen turns black. Press it again, and your last slide comes up. Press "W," and the screen becomes white.

The bulbs in these projectors get very hot. I have seen attorneys prop legal pads in front of the lens or use the lens caps. I have never seen a legal pad catch fire, but lens caps have melted, lenses have cracked, and bulbs worth hundreds of dollars have burst. Use the "B" and "W" keys instead.

9. Use Available Resources

"At the Section Annual Conference this year, W. Mark Lanier, who is a trendsetter in the use of PowerPoint, spoke about using it to present images instead of just words," says John P. Hutchins, Atlanta, GA, co-Director of the Section of Litigation's Division IV–Procedural and former cochair of the Section of Litigation's Technology for the Litigator Committee. "He has revolutionized the way it is used at trial."

10. Don't Get Carried Away

Trust me, this can be fun. However, you can get carried away. The last thing you want is one of the jurors coming up to you at the end of your trial and asking, "How did you get the little arrows to fly in?" You want the jury concentrating on substance, not form.

People usually get carried away with colors and animations. Presentation software includes many animations that can be distracting. My go-to buttons for animation are "fade" and "appear" as opposed to say, "pinwheel." Try "pinwheel," and you will see what I mean. Good luck.

Resources:

Sample PowerPoint Presentation *available at* http://bit.ly/sample-powerpoint.

W. Mark Lanier, "Constructing the Ultimate PowerPoint," *available at* http://bit.ly/ABA-SAC-powerpoint.

The Power of Simplicity

"I should be glad, if I could flatter myself that I came as near to the central idea of the occasion, in two hours, as you did in two minutes." So wrote Edward Everett to Abraham Lincoln the day after the Gettysburg Address.

Edward Everett, the principal speaker at Gettysburg, was a congressman, senator, governor of Massachusetts, minister to Great Britain, secretary of state, president of Harvard, and considered to be a spellbinding orator. At Gettysburg, he spoke for two hours. We don't remember a single word.

Lincoln was mistaken that "the world will little note, nor long remember what we say here." The world has certainly both noted and long remembered what he said at Gettysburg. There is genius in simplicity. Less is truly more. Albert Einstein said, "If you can't explain it simply, you don't understand it well enough."

I'm still not sure what happens to us or when it happens to us. Perhaps at a young age we were rewarded for knowing big words. Perhaps we got A's in vocabulary or won a spelling bee. Most likely, it happens our first year of law school when we want to write or sound like our perception of a lawyer.

A few years ago, a first-year law student called to ask me for help securing an externship. His purpose in calling me was for connection, not correction. However, when I asked that he send his résumé so that I could include it in a letter of introduction, the corrections were necessary. I simply could not have him send his résumé to any of my colleagues.

Now know that this young man was very bright: Ivy League law school, top of his class at undergrad, and an Eagle Scout to boot. Under "Experience" he listed working as a certified pharmacy technician. Being able to deal with people is an important asset.

However, this was his description of the job: "Facilitated customer satisfaction and insured patient retention through detailed explanation and complaint resolution." I told him to change it to: "Helped customers." Any judge worth working for appreciates clear, simple language. If you can say it in two words, why use thirteen? He got the job.

Let's turn to the courtroom. Two years ago I was asked to speak at an advocacy institute. I like to sit in on the other lectures, and in one of them, a judge was retelling what she considered to be one of the shortest, but most powerful openings she had ever heard.

She asked both counsel if they were ready to proceed, and they were. She gave the green light to the plaintiff's attorney, and as he was rising he said, "May it please the court." He then paused, all attention upon him, and said these five words: "Your Honor—the roof leaks." And he sat down.

The judge said it was the most brilliant opening statement she had ever heard. He captured the essence of the case in three words, and she said defense counsel was backpedaling from there on.

It does take courage to trust that a laser beam is better than a blunderbuss. Where does this come from? As lawyers we are trained to dot every "i" and cross every "t." However, when I send out jury surveys, the number one complaint about lawyers is that they are too repetitious. It is as if we do not trust that people understand us unless we repeat ourselves multiple times.

What may be a good argument loses impact if it is repeated over and over again. The listener begins to wonder why the speaker keeps plowing the same ground. Good arguments are not subject to the same formula as recipes. Twice the salt makes the dish twice as salty. In my opinion, stating the exact same thing twice makes it half as good.

While "of the people, by the people, for the people" is both beautiful and persuasive, "of the people, of the people, of the people" is not. Repetition can be powerful if there is some variation to it, but it is boring if not varied, and, in some instances, it can actually hurt our case.

"I find the less experienced the attorney, the longer the cross, which is usually a real mistake," says Hon. Nancy Friedman Atlas, Houston, TX, cochair of the ABA Section of Litigation's Federal Practice Task Force. "Restrict yourself to points that are strong. Juries think that arguing with witnesses is a waste of time. Save the argument for closing."

Now, let's turn to the power of simplicity in writing. The following two sentences were taken from a 1949 U.S. Supreme Court decision reversing a murder conviction based on a coerced confession. Justice Felix Frankfurter wrote: "[T]his was a calculated endeavor to secure a confession through the pressure of unrelenting interrogation." Justice Douglas wrote: "The man was held until he broke."

Those two sentences say exactly the same thing. Justice Douglas's sentence has the power of simplicity. It would be the perfect opening line to a motion to suppress, an opening statement, or an argument on appeal: "This is a case . . . about a man . . . who was held . . . until he broke." Say it out loud, pausing for the periods, to hear the power of this sentence.

Simplicity also helps us handle the bad stuff. An old adage among trial lawyers is that if you don't have the law, pound the facts; if you don't have the facts, pound the law; and if you have neither, pound the table. I have read some articles on advocacy that advise making the case more complicated or obtuse if both the law and facts are against you. I think this is bad advice.

Your credibility with a judge is everything. If both the law and the facts are against you, do you really think you can trick the judge into thinking something simple is truly complex? If you are faced with this dilemma, is there another way that preserves your credibility and serves your client?

I tell new attorneys that the shortest distance between law school and earning the respect of judges is strict adherence to ABA Model Rule of Professional Conduct 3.3(a)(2), which states "A lawyer shall not knowingly fail to disclose to the tribunal authority in the controlling jurisdiction known to the lawyer to be directly adverse to the position of the client and not disclosed by opposing counsel."

In fact, I tell new attorneys to take the words "directly adverse" and change them to "arguably adverse." Why? There is nothing more powerful than the advocate who comes into court and says, "Your Honor, this is our position. However, we must tell you there are three cases that are arguably against us. Here they are. Here is the one case in our favor, and we would ask the court to follow it for the following reasons."

There is power in simply and quickly separating the wheat from the chaff for the court. There is power in total frankness on both the facts and the law, and there is power in citing contrary authority. You show you are not concerned about it. It is even more devastating for the other side when you cite cases that are against you that they have not found. No less an advocate than Cicero said that the perfect advocate is one who can argue both sides of any case.

Judges learn very quickly which advocates tell them the truth, the whole truth, and nothing but the truth. You are going to have cases with bad facts and law that is against you. In these cases, your battle is all uphill. Frankly telling the court, "Your Honor, the law is against us, however . . ." or "We are going to ask the court today to go out on a limb and find this provision does not apply, or is void, or is unconstitutional for these reasons . . ." gets our attention and has power. Total frankness with the court and hitting your obstacles head on, combined with citing contrary authority, builds your reputation as an ethical and effective advocate.

It is fitting that I end with closing argument. "Short words are the best," said Winston Churchill, "...and old words when short are the best of all." Short words, well said, have power.

Although the pedigree of the following story can be questioned, the point cannot. According to literary urban legend, Ernest Hemingway was sitting with some fellow writers at The Round Table at the Algonquin Hotel. A challenge was issued as to who could evoke the most emotion with the fewest words. Wagers were placed. Hemingway took a napkin and wrote these words: "For sale, baby shoes, never worn." Hemingway collected his winnings.

"I recall reading about a less than two-minute closing argument delivered by the late great Moe Levine for a client who had lost both arms," recalls Paul Mark Sandler, Baltimore, MD, cochair of the Section's Litigation Institute for Trial Training. "His final two lines were: 'I need not call any army of experts and parade before you countless medical professionals to illustrate this boy's loss. I need only tell you that I had lunch with him today . . . and he ate his food . . . like a dog.'"

Resources:

Watts v. Indiana, 338 U.S. 49 (1949).

Steven Wisotsky, *Speaking with Power and Style* (2013).

Is Technology Changing Our Brains?

"The year was 2081, and everybody was finally equal. They weren't only equal before God and the law. They were equal every which way. Nobody was smarter than anybody else. Nobody was better looking than anybody else. Nobody was stronger or quicker than anybody else. All this equality was due to the 211th, 212th, and 213th Amendments to the Constitution, and to the unceasing vigilance of agents of the United States Handicapper General."

And so begins Kurt Vonnegut's short story, *Harrison Bergeron*. The story opens with George and Hazel (husband and wife) watching a ballet on television. However, the ballerinas wear weights, so they are not too graceful, and masks, so they are not too beautiful.

Vonnegut then describes the couple: "Hazel had a perfectly average intelligence, which meant she couldn't think about anything except in short bursts. And George, while his intelligence was way above normal, had a little mental handicap radio in his ear. He was required by law to wear it at all times. It was tuned to a government transmitter. Every twenty seconds or so, the transmitter would send out some sharp noise to keep people like George from taking unfair advantage of their brains."

After reading *Harrison Bergeron*, I have three questions: (1) In 2015, have we reached Vonnegut's vision of the year 2081—66 years early? (2) Have we self-inflicted Vonnegut's vision of repeated interruptions by our own addiction to technology? (3) If so, what difference does this make to us as advocates and judges?

Research shows that, on the average, people check their cellphones 150 times per day. That average goes up dramatically the younger you are. The average cellphone owner uses their phone 3 hours and 16 minutes every day. These statistics are just for cellphone use alone. They do not cover those people who sit at a computer all day receiving e-mails and instant messaging.

So, what happens when we take people out of the real world and put them in a courtroom without access to their phones? In the real world, they would, on average, be checking their phone every 6 1/2 minutes. What happens when a person is forced to go cold turkey from technology?

Let's look at some studies. Many studies have been conducted on depriving college students of their cellphones. These are our next generation of jurors. The students reported symptoms similar to addicts trying to quit smoking or taking drugs. The condition now has a name. It is Information Deprivation Disorder.

Ask yourself some questions. Is it easier or harder for you to concentrate on reading a brief, or a case, than it was just 10 years ago? Have you ever gotten into a car to go to a movie and told your companion that you needed to go back inside to grab your cellphone. Why? You're going to a movie!

Moreover, even if we take cellphones away from jurors, the mere thought of those text messages piling up in the jury room, or in their car outside the courthouse, can be just as distracting.

A researcher wrote, "The problem is that just because a student's technology is 'out of sight' it is not 'out of mind.' For example, [one study] found no neurological differences between externally driven task switching (e.g., responding to a text message beep) and internally driven switches (e.g., 'thinking about' a text message)."

Brain scientists have known for years that our brains are constantly changing. The brain adapts and finds new pathways when the brain is damaged or when the person learns a new skill, such as a new language or playing the piano. Our brains also change based upon whether the information received is primarily verbal or visual, and how many times the information being received is interrupted.

Studies have shown that when a person is interrupted from doing a task, the time it takes to get back on task is from a low of 15 minutes to a high of 25 minutes. In the real world, people are constantly being distracted by information technology. Moreover, the distraction is usually visual preceded by an auditory "Bing!" from their device.

In the real world, the information is usually chopped into bits (texts and Twitter), given at random, unpredictable intervals and is visual. In the courtroom, the information is more linear. It is continuous and flowing, and it is mostly verbal. This is a big shift for the brain.

That's the bad news. Now, here's the good news. When people are told about the phenomena of being interrupted, and the effect those interruptions have on concentration, they are able to adapt and improve their performance. So, how do we tell them? How do we address this issue to counteract Information Deprivation Disorder?

I suggest three fixes. First, address it head on. Second, see if the judge will let the jurors ask questions. Third, do what the great trial lawyers have done for years. Both show and tell the jury about your case and, if you have to rely totally on verbal information, become a master at delivering that information by chunking it.

Let's say you have three-week trial looming, involving forensic accounting or gene sequencing or thermodynamics. There are three experts on each side. You know, under the local rule, no cellphones are allowed in the courthouse. Address that elephant in the room head on.

Questions such as, "Folks, we estimate this will take about three weeks. It will involve a lot of science. We know you cannot bring your cellphones into the courthouse and the judge has already told you that you cannot use your phone to do independent research. So, will leaving your cellphone in your car be so much of a distraction for any of you that it would be hard for you to listen to the evidence in this case?"

In my opinion, this accomplishes three things. First, some jurors may be honest enough to admit that it would cause a problem. They are probably the ones who post more than ten times a day, every day, such crucial information as, "The line is sooooo long at Starbucks this morning! (sad face)" You must then decide whether the other attributes of that juror outweigh the juror's concern about the world not knowing how long the line is at the local Starbucks.

Second, once you talk about the elephant in the room, the elephant becomes smaller, or may even disappear. The brain scientists tell us that when people are alerted to the phenomena, they are better able to handle it.

Third, even if the cellphone addicted juror does not come forward, their fellow jurors may alert the court if that juror is either not deliberating in good faith, or directly violates a court rule and brings their cellphone in the jury room. Judges have the option of removing jurors for misconduct and putting in an alternate juror.

Next, propose to the court that the jurors be allowed to submit questions. The ancient Chinese proverb says, "Tell me and I'll forget; show me and I may remember; involve me and I'll understand." This may turn the passive jurors who are sitting there thinking about all the texts they are not reading, or all of the events they are not posting, into more active, listening jurors. Peer dynamics can be powerful, especially if others are submitting questions.

Finally, how can we make the information that flows in court more like the information they are used to in the real world? Fortunately, great trial lawyers have used these techniques for years. They show, as well as tell, the jury about their case and they are masters at delivering verbal information.

The brain scientists tell us that people remember 70–80% of what they both see and hear and only about 10–15% of what they just hear. Great trial lawyers show their cases to their juries. A picture truly is worth a thousand words.

If the scene is important, introduce a picture early so that the witness can show the jury the scene. If dates are important, make sure the witness doesn't merely regurgitate when things happened, prepare a diagram or flow chart to use with the witness or maybe as early as opening statement. The great trial attorneys are always asking, "I want them to hear this information, but how can I also show it?"

I am running out of space. So, what if all you have are words? Listen to the Rev. Martin Luther King deliver a speech. Listen to David Boies argue or make an announcement at a press conference. They are masters of pausing and delivering discrete, meaningful chunks of information. Kinda like a good tweet.

Resources:

Kurt Vonnegut, Jr., *Harrison Bergeron* (1961).

Larry D. Rosen, Alex F. Lim, L. Mark Carrier, and Nancy A. Cheever, "An Empirical Examination of the Educational Impact of Text Message-Induced Task Switching in the Classroom: Educational Implications and Strategies to Enhance Learning" *Psicologia Educativa*, Vol. 17, n.2, p. 163–177 (2011).

Bob Sullivan and Hugh Thompson, "Brain, Interrupted," *New York Times*, May 3, 2013.

Richard Gray, "Facebook Generation Suffer Information Withdrawal Syndrome," *The Telegraph*, January 2, 2011.

Mark A. Drummond, "How About a Free Shadow Jury? Inside the Juror's Mind," *Litigation News*, Vol. 38, No. 2 at 16 (Winter 2013).

John R. Stegner, "Of Course Jurors Should Ask Questions. Lessons Learned from 16 Years on the Trial Bench," *Litigation News*, Vol. 38, No. 4 at 20 (Summer 2013).

CHAPTER 4

WITNESS EXAMINATION

Panning for Gold: A Depositions Roundtable

The phone rings and you reach for it. The voice on the other end says, "Could I see you in my office?" You pad down the corridor and replay that one sentence in your mind. As you round the corner into her office, you see that she is holding a transcript of the deposition you took last week for the trial that begins next month. The furrow on her brow matches her inflection on the phone. Perhaps the two most feared questions that associates who take depositions face from trial partners are "Why didn't you ask this?" or "Why didn't you follow up on that?"

Because fewer than 5 percent of all cases go to trial, and because most of our time is spent in discovery, I thought I would brainstorm some "nuts and bolts" techniques for depositions with the three former ABA Section of Litigation cochairs of the Pretrial Practice and Discovery Committee: Erica L. Calderas, Cleveland; Ian H. Fisher, Chicago; and Kent A. Lambert, New Orleans.

Distilling the nearly half-century of experience of these three into a top 10 list, we defined our deposition goals:

What do they know?
What don't they know?
If they don't know, who or what does?
Cut off escape routes at trial.
Size them up for trial.
Size up opposing counsel for trial.
Gather support for motions to dismiss, summary judgment, etc.
Get facts for requests to admit.
Get clean admissions for cross.
Find where you need to direct supplemental discovery.

With these goals in mind, let's go to our three experts for some practical tips. "First, know the rules," says Fisher. "There aren't that many rules, so one should know them, especially unique local rules. For example, in state court in Illinois, we maintain a distinction between evidence and discovery depositions and how they can be used. We have a time limit of three hours for discovery depositions. It can be a nasty surprise to the lawyer from New York when the Illinois lawyer stands up and says, 'Well, it's been three hours and 10 minutes, so see you around." The judge may or may not give you an extension, but that would involve a request, a hearing, and another trip, or two, back to Illinois.

Once you know the rules, "Start with the basics by focusing on the elements of the claims and defenses," counsels Calderas. "Have a checklist or outline of those elements to remind you of your focus."

"I organize my outline so I have one topic per page or group of pages," adds Lambert. "This way I can, on the fly, reorder the topics if the witness jumps to something that I otherwise intended to do at the end of the day. Written outlines are important, but I do not want to become tied to them unless there are 'terms of art' or very specific questions I want to ask in an exact manner."

"The best deposition outline in the world will not help you if you do not adapt to the witness's responses and conduct follow-up questioning," says Fisher. "Listen, listen, listen is the most important, and often most ignored, rule. I just read a deposition taken by another attorney where the witness's answer was, 'Well, as you have asked the question, my answer is no.' The attorney moved on. That witness had just hung a big red flag on that answer." The natural follow-up question would have been "So how should I have asked it so your answer is 'Yes.'"

"As an example, let's say you ask the broad question of who was at a particular meeting and the response is 'Well, Bob was there,'" offers Lambert. "You then ask, 'Well, who else was there?'" until you exhaust the witness's memory and he or she responds "No one else was there other than the people I named."

Now the problem with this exchange is that it may take three pages of questions and answers to pin the witness down to who was at the meeting. However, you need one clean answer for trial that you can use.

Remember that the nuggets of gold that you are pulling out of the deposition are separate and discrete pieces that do not have the context of the entire deposition. It is like a movie. You must make sure the clip you are showing the jury is complete, in context, and understandable. They were not at the deposition.

"Always think about the record you are making," says Calderas. "I've seen records where counsel thought he was getting a nice clean sound bite only to see later that the testimony was riddled with objections, the witness talking over him, and half-stated questions with no foundation laid."

"Go see a cross-examination and see how questions are asked and how people use transcripts to impeach," adds Lambert. "Until you see and understand how you are going to use it, you don't understand how to ask the questions. What you need at the end of the day are direct 'yes/no' answers in the transcript and you may have to ask the question a couple of times to wheedle them down to the ultimate answer."

So, in our meeting example, our goal would be to take the names that came out in the three pages and extract a simple "Yes" response to a question such as, "So, the only people at the meeting at Acme on March 12, 2006, were Bob S., Susan R., Phil H., and you?"

"Think about what the transcript will look like," adds Fisher. "Be sure and refer to exhibits with specificity, avoid using pronouns, non-verbal communication, humor, or sarcasm. They don't translate well into the record." Everyone in the deposition may know who "He" or "She" is because you have been talking about that person for the last half hour, but at trial if you want to pull the admission "He was drunk" out of the deposition, you need "his" name, especially if there were one hundred other people at the party.

"You have to start broad because you don't know the answers, but you have to funnel this broad information down to something useable for trial," says Lambert. "As an examiner, you must practice asking the follow-up questions that get the complete answer and foreclose future additional testimony," adds Calderas.

What if, in our example, the witness responds that he does not remember or does not know? Do you stop there? "Normally I would ask them if there is anything that would refresh their recollection," says Lambert.

Ask if there is any document that would remind them, any other person who would know, any and all sources they could go to find the information they claim that they do not know or cannot remember. You can listen to an audio clip of Professor James McElhaney's 14 suggested follow-up questions to the answer "I don't know" at the ABA bookstore.

"Opposing counsel sometimes become human Geiger counters," continues Fisher. "As I get near something that is good, then the rate of objections start to increase, they get more and more excited, and, on a few occasions, I have actually found my way into admissions that I might not otherwise have found."

Look for clues from opposing counsel and the deponent. Slowing down on answers and injecting qualifiers are two such clues. "If I ask the question 'Do you always do X?' and they respond 'On Tuesdays we do X,' that is a qualified response that needs to be explored," advises Fisher. "Written outlines are important, but do not become so tied to them that you miss qualifiers, inflections, and other cues for follow-up questions."

Finally, if the personnel you encounter on your way to court like you, that can be a definite plus. "I once took a deposition where the fellow would literally write down every question I asked, write out his answer to it, and then read it out loud," shares Lambert. "During a break, the court reporter volunteered that she could run the time in the margin and I said, 'Please do.'" This would certainly defeat any claim at trial that the deponent was rushed.

Most good depositions are like panning for gold. You sift through a lot to get a little and then protect what you've got for trial. As you pan for the gold, realize that everyone in that room is sizing you up. Are you able to get the crucial facts? Can you distill them down to a usable form? Can you cut off escape routes for trial, and, ultimately, can you try a case?

Resources:

Jerold S. Solovy & Robert L. Byman, "Discovery-Wacky Rules", *Nat'l L.J.*, Aug. 25, 2008.

James W. McElhaney, *McElhaney's Deposition Notebook*, (ABA 2003), available from the ABA Web Store at www.ababooks.org or (800) 285-2221.

Thinking Ahead on Impeachment

Commandment Seven of Professor Irving Younger's Ten Commandments of Cross-Examination is: Do not permit the witness to explain. We can do this in U.S. courts. We can impeach with a prior inconsistent statement, and should the witness blurt out an explanation, we can ask that it be stricken.

However, some judicial systems require that the witness be given the opportunity to explain. Why the difference? Is there any circumstance under which we would violate Professor Younger's Seventh Commandment?

In 2009, I was working with attorneys in Kosovo. While teaching impeachment, I was told that they are required to ask the witness to explain the inconsistency. Their criminal code requires that either the judge or the parties ask the witness to explain why he or she is testifying differently.

Similarly, British barristers are required to "Put their case to the witness." In other words, the witness's attention must first be drawn to a particular point on the basis of which it is intended to suggest that he is not speaking the truth, and thereafter the witness must be afforded an opportunity to explain. If the proposition is not "put to" the witness, the barrister is barred from arguing that the witness's testimony should be rejected.

British books on advocacy always stress the barrister's duty of fairness to the witness on cross, whereas our system allows us to cut off, or have stricken, the explanation. We can just let the witness twist in the wind. Fairness comes from the redirect. But, are there any instances where we might want to adopt the other approach? Is the impeachment of the 80-year-old, unbiased occurrence witness different from the impeachment of the $1,000-per-hour expert?

Let's go back. The case is at trial. You know through discovery that you have impeaching documents.

First of all, let's look at the basic skill of impeachment with a prior inconsistent statement. At the very minimum, an advocate must know how to:

- commit the witness to what he or she said in court
- credit the prior statement in the jurors' eyes as the true version of the facts
- confront the witness with the prior statement

At National Institute for Trial Advocacy training courses, we call it "The Three Cs—Commit, Credit, and Confront."

I prefer what I call the "parental commitment." In an incredulous tone, the witness is asked, "Now Mr. Jones, did you just tell this jury that the light was red for the westbound Chevrolet?" It is said in the same tone that I use with my children: "Alexander, did I just hear you tell your mother that I said you could go?"

This can be paired with a follow-up question, stating the version you actually believe to be true: "Now Mr. Jones, isn't it true that the light was green for the westbound Chevrolet?" The witness has now admitted that he made the first statement to the jury and has flatly denied the second statement.

Then you credit the previous statement with as much as you need to show to the jury that this is more likely the truth. If it was under oath, great; if they signed it, fantastic; if the other attorney was there; if they corrected it; if it was given to law enforcement—anything that tells the jury that the prior statement is the truth.

Then comes confrontation. The attorney takes the statement to the witness. If it is a deposition, give the page and line number to opposing counsel. If it is a statement, give the page and line number to opposing counsel. Why? When you are bearing down on their witness, opposing counsel will look for any opportunity to interrupt with "Your honor, we don't know what counsel is referring to."

You then get the witness to admit that this is his or her statement and those are his or her words. You do not settle for "I guess" or "If you say so." You must extract an unequivocal "Yes" to "This is your statement, and those are your words."

Be sure that you read the statement. Trust me, you will read it better than the witness will. Once he or she admits that you read his or her words correctly, you are done under our system. You are not required to ask the witness to explain the inconsistency.

But does it end there? What happens in a real courtroom? The first thing that can happen is that the other side can try to pull the teeth out of your cross by impeaching their own witness on direct. If it is a big discrepancy, they may try to bring it out on voir dire. They will tell the jurors that a witness they are calling has told two versions and ask the jurors if they will keep an open mind until they hear the explanation. They may admit in their opening statement that there are two versions.

If they have done some type of preemptive strike before your cross, then the commitment and the confrontation have essentially been done for you. Most preemptive strikes involve discrediting the prior statement usually on some grounds such as confusion by the witness, vagueness of the statement, or further reflection by the witness. Generally, then your goal on cross is to re-credit the previous statement.

But let's say they don't pull out the teeth. You impeach and the witness either says: "Yes I said that, but . . ." and blurts out an explanation, or asks: "May I explain?" The safest, and usually correct, answer is "NO !" You don't let the witness explain. You reject the offer to explain with a polite, but firm, "No, thank you." If the witness blurts it out, you must consider what you do in light of: how you wish to appear to the jury; the witness—whether he or she is a paid expert, impartial, or biased, and the impeaching statement itself.

Your options are three in number: erase it, ignore it, or address it. You can ask the judge to erase it; to strike everything after "Yes, I said that"; to instruct the jury to disregard it (Pay no attention to the man behind the curtain!); and to admonish the witness to just answer the question. In my experience, admonishment usually only falls upon the paid expert who should know better, and rarely on the unbiased occurrence witness. In any event, you must weigh the effect of erasure on the jury. Does it make you appear afraid of the witness or afraid of the explanation? Can you unring the bell?

David Berg has an entire section in his book of advocacy, *The Trial Lawyer: What It Takes to Win* (ABA 2006), entitled "(Never Ignore) Offers to Explain." Berg offers advice on how to handle offers to explain and cautions about appearing to be afraid of explanations. Remember, you are playing to the jury, and in their lives, if someone offers an explanation, it is usually polite to hear the person out.

Ignoring the explanation or the offer to explain also communicates something to the jury. It can be construed as if the explanation does not matter, but it can also come off as rude. Many attorneys just choose to ignore it because they know they will have the last word in closing argument.

British barristers must address it. Addressing it involves risk. Generally, the more facts or opinions in a statement, the more risk. The witness has more room to wiggle. The statement "The Hummer had the red light" carries less risk than the statement "From where I was, I thought the car was going a little bit over the speed limit."

"If you know any explanation for the inconsistent statement will be totally implausible, why not let them [explain]?" asks Jeffrey L. Willis, Tucson, member of the Section of Litigation's Access to Justice Committee. "This is just further impeachment. This would be especially so if there are prior statements inconsistent with the explanation, which could provide an opportunity for impeachment."

"In the case of an initially disinterested witness, I would think that asking for an explanation might be advisable if his courtroom testimony was unfavorable and there has been some intervening event such as considerable contact with opposing counsel before the trial," adds Willis. "Other than those two exceptions, I would not ask for an explanation because this is not required."

The additional advantage of not addressing it in your cross is that it gives you the chance to watch jury reaction if they redirect on the inconsistency. Shaking heads, suppressed smiles, or downturned eyes can tell you a lot about whether the jurors are buying it. This is harder to gauge if you are the one asking the questions. You may then choose to address it on re-cross or just save it for comment in closing.

What's the answer to the question of how to handle the explanation? The answer is: "It depends." After all, trying cases is an art, not a science.

Resource:

David Berg, *The Trial Lawyer: What It Takes to Win* (ABA 2006); *available at* http://shop.americanbar.org/eBus/Store/ProductDetails.aspx?productId=214881.

Defending Depositions: Know the Rules, Written and Unwritten

Before reading this article, please go to your favorite Internet search engine, type in the words "Old Lawyer Fight," and sit back and watch. I'll wait until you're done.

Good, you're back. If you have not seen this before, I would guess that this video is probably the most viewed video on lawyer behavior in a deposition. Obviously, the camera did not affect behavior.

Most new lawyers will first defend a deposition before they take a deposition. What Section of Litigation resources are available to the young lawyer who might be heading to defend his or her first deposition? The three former cochairs for the Section's Pretrial Practice and Discovery Committee, Betsy P. Collins, Atlanta; Ian H. Fisher, Chicago; and Kent A. Lambert, New Orleans, offer some practical advice.

You must first determine whether the person you are taking to the deposition is "your client." If he or she is a person and has retained you, then the person is your client.But what if you are representing a corporate defendant? Is every person who works for the corporation a "client" covered by the attorney-client privilege? You need to know before the deposition, and that answer may depend on the state or federal law in that particular jurisdiction.

Seeking agreements with opposing counsel on just who they consider to be "clients" for the purpose of defending may help solve problems in the deposition. However, just because you and opposing counsel agree, does not necessarily mean that it is wise for you to assume the role of defending counsel for every witness on your "side" of the case. It is crucial to have a clear understanding on who is "the client" and to anticipate possible conflicts in multiple witness cases.

Next, "Always, always read the relevant rules, including the local rules and standing orders," says Fisher. "In Illinois state court, discovery depositions are limited to 3 hours and some jurisdictions severely restrict the right to consult with counsel during a deposition. Know the rules on objections—the ones that must be made or they are waived," he says.

In addition to the Federal Rules of Civil Procedure, 18 federal district courts have adopted local rules regarding the defender's role in such areas as conferences with the client, speaking objections, and justifying on the record an instruction not to answer. Going deeper, there may be deposition rules that are imposed by a particular judge or standing orders that apply to a particular case.

"If you are going into a foreign jurisdiction, always call a local practitioner to learn both the written and, perhaps, unwritten rules," counsels Fisher. "You need to find out what they mean by the phrase usually said at the beginning of every deposition: 'Usual stipulations counselor?'" Those "usual" stipulations vary from place to place, Fisher notes.

Once you are confident on the rules and local practice, you can better prepare the client for what to expect regarding their role, your role, your objections, conferences, and their obligation to answer, except when directed by you not to answer.

"Not feeling prepared was one common complaint I heard when people returned from their deposition," recalls Collins from her days as in-house counsel. "I always wanted the witness to be prepared on what documents they might see at the deposition, although I know not all attorneys share that belief under the theory that this might lead to questions on what the witness was shown in preparation and how deep they can delve into that varies so much from jurisdiction to jurisdiction."

"It depends on the case but, if it is early in the case, there are some core documents that your witness ought to know," adds Lambert. "But, if they show your witness a new document, you need to make sure to take the time for both of you to review it before the questions start."

"You need to know the rule or local practice on whether you can talk to the witness, whether it be a client or not, during the breaks," adds Collins.

"I know of some jurisdictions where counsel take the position that, once the witness is sworn, all communication is fair game except that related to a discussion of privilege. You might want to set the ground rules by agreement with opposing counsel, in advance, to avoid problems."

"You need to know whether your preparation is privileged or not," says Fisher. "Just because you prepared a witness, does not mean you are the witness's attorney. Carefully consider your obligations to your current client before agreeing to represent a non-party witness and remember the number one admonition to all witnesses: 'Tell the truth.'"

"Be sure to go over the mechanics with your witness," continues Fisher. "Explain to them the types of questions that will be asked, that they should not speculate and the strange fact that they will have to answer many questions, even after you have objected."

After you have prepared the witness, you must prepare your game plan on objections. A common myth under the federal rules is that all objections, except as to form, are preserved. "Actually, it is the 'no ambush' rule," says Fisher. "If it can be cured at the deposition, the rules say that it should be made there. But just because you can object does not mean that you should. Sometimes you are better off leaving a muddled question alone and speaking objections are unprofessional and rarely accomplish their goal."

You should plan to arrive early so neither of you feel rushed. Be sure to bring your card. Nothing is more embarrassing than all of the other lawyers doing the pro forma tossing of the card to the court reporter only for you to realize, in front of your client, that you forgot to bring one. You might as well tattoo "Rookie" on your forehead.

Never leave your client alone. People never want to appear unfriendly, and your client may be tempted to engage in casual conversation that might prove detrimental down the road. Make sure they know that they can take breaks when needed and can have refreshments while testifying. Finally, let them know that there may be disputes that are just part of the process.

"It has been my experience that in 98 percent of the cases there may be a lot of posturing on these issues, but very little resolution," says Collins. "It is hard to know the local practice, since they may go as far as to call a judge to get a ruling, but that rarely appears in a reported opinion that lawyers can reference."

"I always take the judge's phone number with me to the deposition," says Fisher. "I have threatened on six occasions to make the phone call and actually made the call on one occasion. In each case, it solved the problem. You might want to sound the judge out on whether they will take calls to resolve issues. I have had judges who have volunteered to be available to solve problems, rather than risk that the lawyers will suspend the deposition."

Although videotaping the deposition may cause everyone to be on his or her best behavior, with some exceptions, the visual element adds to the defender's to-do list. "I always look through the viewfinder to see how my witness is framed up," counsels Lambert.

Research reveals that how we view information may be as important or, in some cases, more important than what is said. For example, one study in the criminal arena revealed that the simple change from a wide shot of both the interrogator and the suspect, to a narrow shot of the suspect only, doubled the "conviction" rate. What a person wears, camera angle, and lighting all make a difference in Hollywood. The same applies to depositions.

"A witness who does not make eye contact with the camera or a poorly lit witness may not seem credible," says Fisher. "Make sure you also check how your witness sounds on the video. The videographer should help with this. Their microphone may need to be adjusted."

"Videotaping the deposition has an impact on both the witness and the lawyers," notes Lambert. "However, after a while, you and your witness will forget the camera is even there and that is why people love to load up the end of the deposition. You need to make sure your witness gets breaks, especially late in the day when mistakes are likely to be made. I never let my witness go without lunch."

Resources:

Stewart W. Gold & Henry L. Hecht, *Defending at a Deposition* (ABA 2010).

Henry L. Hecht, *Effective Depositions, Second Edition* (ABA 2010).

James W. McElhaney, *McElhaney's Deposition Notebook* (ABA 2003).

Steven Lubet, *Showing Your Hand: A Counter-Intuitive Strategy for Deposition Defense.*

The resources listed above are available from the ABA Web Store at www.ababooks.org or by calling 1-800-285-2221.

Sharon Begley, "Video Cameras, Too, Can Lie, or at Least Create Jury Prejudice", *Wall Street J.*, Jan. 31, 2003.

Sometimes It Pays to Be Underestimated: How to Do an Effective Cross without Resorting to Rambo Tactics

Great advocates are not one-trick ponies. When it comes to cross-examination, they have the ability to—paraphrasing Shakespeare—fit the cross to the witness, the witness to the cross. They do not adopt the silverback male approach to each cross-examination. They do not treat the 80-year-old occurrence witness in the same manner as the expert who has never met an opinion he didn't like—for a price.

Women advocates have the added concern that, while a male advocate may be labeled as "aggressive," which is not necessarily a negative term, women may be labeled with more derogatory terms. "It's frustrating that female attorneys have to deal with it, but we do," says Dawn M. Du Verney, Philadelphia, PA, cochair of the ABA Section of Litigation's Criminal Litigation Committee. "As a black female, I have to combat the stereotype of the 'angry black woman,' which adds another layer."

These days, more American advocates may find themselves facing a tribunal that is used to a different style of cross-examination, such as in international arbitration. All attorneys need to know how to do an effective cross without resorting to Rambo tactics. I called on my good friend in England, Peter Lyons, to discuss this approach to cross-examination.

It's called the Code Red scene. Tom Cruise is Lieutenant Kaffee, and he's cross-examining Jack Nicholson. It's supposed to be Colonel Jessep, but it's really Jack.

> It's pretty clear that Kaffee hasn't been trained by NITA.
>
> He is angry: "Colonel Jessep. Did you order the Code Red?"

"You want answers?" yells Jack.
"I think I'm entitled."
"You want answers?"
The lieutenant screams, "I want the truth!"
Nicholson: "You can't handle the truth!"

Then, unfortunately for the cross-examiner, the witness delivers a spellbinding and quite persuasive speech, which lasts for more than a minute. Undaunted, Kaffee shouts the "Did you?" question again and moves menacingly toward the witness.

It works. He gets the "Yes," and Jack growls, "You're damn right I did!"

I teach advocacy. We have all had a Tom Cruise in our classes—well perhaps not in the looks department—but there is often a student who thinks cross-examination should be done Hollywood-style.

Unfortunately, the Cruise routine is seen by lawyers over on this side of the lagoon as typical of American attorneys. I know it's wrong, and you know it's wrong, but perceptions are sometimes difficult to shift.

Choose the Right Technique

Advocates have a number of weapons in their arsenal. As surely as the punishment should fit the crime, lawyers must know which technique is best suited to deal with the behavior of an awkward witness. Choosing the wrong weapon may well backfire on the cross-examiner.

It helps to look at the purpose of cross-examination. Those who are ignorant of effective advocacy think the purpose is to trip the witness up or argue with him until he admits to the murder.

But the first aim is surely to strengthen your client's case by highlighting the good points through the opponent's witness and by presenting facts that the witness will agree with—or at least not dispute. Such constructive cross-examination can also be used to elicit new meanings or new facts. By contrast, shouting at the witness or attacking her credibility is hardly likely to achieve these aims.

The second purpose of cross-examination is to undermine or discredit your opponent's case by showing the witness's evidence is unreliable. If you think about it, the most important policy behind all the rules of evidence is to try to make sure that what is presented to the court is reliable.

You can show a witness's evidence is unreliable in a number of ways: by demonstrating the witness is mistaken, incompetent, lazy, unprepared, lacking authority, speculating, or biased. The list is not exhaustive. These are effective objectives to argue in your closing statement.

But the most prevalent objective in the eyes of the inexperienced lawyer is to show that the witness should not be believed because he or she is lying. A lying witness is a gift to a skillful cross-examiner, but lying witnesses don't come around that often.

In any event, aggression with a lying witness will rarely be effective and could be counterproductive. If a witness has given a false account of something said out of court, then saying quietly to him, "That wasn't true, was it?" is much more powerful than screaming, "You're a liar!"

Well-Mannered but Lethal

The great Norman Birkett K.C. was famous for delivering well-mannered but lethal cross-examinations. His clerk of 20 years, A.E. Bowker, wrote:

> Never once did I know him to enter a court without a perfect thorough knowledge of his brief. Nor can I recall any occasion when he had "words" with the Bench or his opponent. Neither, indeed, can I recollect any witness whom he did not treat with courtesy and politeness, even though he might challenge the evidence they gave.

One of Birkett's regular clients was a newspaper editor named Geoffrey Williamson. He said Birkett "always put on that benevolent rather, silly-ass manner in court; fumbled with his papers, dropped his pencil, and allowed his glasses to fall forward on his nose—that sort of thing. He knew the usefulness of being underestimated."

Dennis Bardens wrote of Birkett:

> An overconfident opponent tends to neglect his defenses. How often have I seen him approach a witness with an air of "I don't quite understand this yet, but I know you'll make it clear" attitude; as

> though by inference he would accept uncritically whatever answer was forthcoming. The witness would fall for it; admission would follow admission, the true significance of each being lost on the witness, until like a thrust with a rapier, Birkett would administer the coup de grace with one final, fatal question.

Birkett thought an advocate should be able to control his temper at all times. In his presidential address to the Holdsworth Club, Birkett stated that the advocate "should be severe when severity is demanded, and he should be gentle when gentleness brings its own rich rewards."

Cross-Examination or Bullying?

This implies that different witnesses and situations call for different styles from the advocate. Whenever I teach in the United States, I am always amused at the students who can't wait to use impeachment as a weapon in cross-examination. They have barely mastered the skill of short, closed questions, and yet there they are, diving for the nuclear button.

I saw one student cross-examining a witness in a traffic case:

> "The light was green?"
> "Well . . ."
> "This isn't the first time you've been asked about this?"

I advised him to let the witness deny it first.

There are many reasons why a witness might be difficult. It could be that the witness misheard or misunderstood the question. Aggressive cross-examination would look like bullying. It may also be that the question is not tight, and the witness can slip through.

In England, where everything that's good was supposedly invented, the bar rules are plain. A barrister is "responsible for the conduct and presentation of his case and must exercise personal judgment upon the substance and purpose of statements made and questions asked" and "must not make statements or ask questions which are merely scandalous or intended only to vilify, insult, or annoy either a witness or some other person."

In his book *The Technique of Advocacy*, John Munkman discusses different styles of cross-examination. He says that successful cross-examination is based on three main techniques: confrontation, probing, and insinuation. Confrontation means presenting the witness with a mass of damaging facts that he cannot deny and that are inconsistent with his evidence. It is appropriate in big cases, but in smaller cases it becomes a method of firm insinuation. Probing means a detailed examination of the story to discover flaws. Insinuation is the creation of a different version of the evidence that strengthens the cross-examiner's case and "draws the sting" from the direct evidence.

Preparation Is Key; Beware the Pitfalls

One should be careful to watch advocates in court and learn from their errors or lapses in style. But it also pays to read widely of skillful advocates from the past. We tend to think we are more civilized because we have computers and television. But the advocates of the past were presented with the same complex human problems.

Remember, first impressions are difficult to shift. The judge and jury make up their minds about advocates in the first 30 seconds. Birkett was renowned for asking clever opening questions. His clerk says he spent days preparing the right form of words.

Being polite does not mean being weak. Still, no matter how hard one tries to be well-mannered, there are pitfalls. Many advocates introduce a cross-examination by mentioning the name of the witness. I taught for the Law Society in Hong Kong a few years ago. Some lawyers in my class had interesting names. A man of 50 was called Peter Pan. Another, playing a witness, was addressed by his cross-examiner, who chose courteously to begin with his name. The effect was not quite what the lawyer had been looking for: "Yiu Lai!"

Resources:

Marcus Stone, *Cross-Examination in Criminal Trials* (3d ed. 2009).

A.E. Bowker, *Behind the Bar* (1947).

Dennis Bardens, *Lord Justice Birkett* (1962).

Richard Du Cann, *The Art of the Advocate* (1993).

Making Experts Come Alive

I believe expert testimony is like salami. It is most appetizing served very thinly. I also believe there are two hurdles to expert testimony. The first hurdle is for you to convince the jury that your expert is simply a better expert than the other expert. The second hurdle is for the jury to actually understand the math, medicine, physics, or chemistry behind your expert's opinion and agree with that opinion.

Although it is impossible to cover the direct examination of experts from A to Z in a 1,500-word article, I think I can boil it down to some fundamentals.

The structure I learned through teaching for the National Institute for Trial Advocacy is as follows: (1) introduction, (2) teaser, (3) qualifications, (4) tender (if required), (5) opinion, (6) basis, (7) source of information, (8) differences with other expert(s) and why, and (9) anticipate cross.

The introduction is simply, "Doctor, would you introduce yourself to the jury." The teaser is, "Doctor Jones, are you in court today to testify to a reasonable degree of medical certainty (or probability depending on your standard) as to the cause of Mr. Smith's seizures?"

The purpose of the teaser question is to orient the jury as to why the expert is in court. It does not contain the opinion, only the topic. The example I used was a single issue examination. If the expert is going to give multiple opinions, then the teaser includes all of those parts. You then tick off, by number, the topics of the opinions he or she is going to give.

The numbering of the opinions achieves two goals. First, people who study the brain tell us that we process words in a different part of the brain than we process numbers. Listing the opinion topics by number makes the brain work harder, and the jury pays more attention.

The second reason is more homespun, but it involves the oft-told story of the famous minister who was once asked why his sermons were so popular. His response was, "Because I give the sermon three times. I tell 'em what I'm going to tell 'em, then I tell 'em, then I tell 'em what I told 'em." A very good structure for both sermons and the direct examination of experts.

The next step is, "Professor, before getting to those opinions I want to ask you some questions about your qualifications." When going through qualifications you must—feign interest! The reason I address this with a bit of sarcasm is due to my courtroom experience of seeing attorneys who tend to slough off qualifications because they want to get to the meat of the case.

It is my impression that many times the battle of experts is either won or lost on qualifications. If one expert has better credentials, more experience, taught others, written books on the subject, etc., I always envisioned some jurors thinking, "Well, I am still not sure if I understand the math, medicine, physics, or chemistry, but what I do know is that she is simply a better expert than the other expert."

While we are on the topic of qualifications, let's turn to tactics. If the other side's expert has better qualifications, you may want to stipulate to qualifications rather than let the jury hear every jot and tittle. If the other side accepts your stipulation and moves on, that is probably a mistake.

Although one might think the jury appreciates an attorney's decision to move on, that is usually because the attorney is doing a poor job on qualifications. I have seen attorneys do an excellent job of making qualifications come alive. Jurors pay as much attention to witnesses as you do.

If you go through qualifications in a dry, pro forma, rote manner, it will not make much of an impact. However, if you appear interested, the jury will pay attention. I have seen experts give interesting and even moving answers to questions such as, "Doctor, tell us why you decided to pick orthopedics as a specialty?" Many have fascinating reasons why they chose their field, and almost any answer other than "the money" is a good answer.

If you have the better expert and the other side tries to shortcut qualifications by stipulating, try to politely decline with a simple statement such as, "Although we appreciate counsel's stipulation that Dr. Jones is qualified to testify on these topics, we believe the jury should hear those qualifications." If the judge pressures you to move on, an effective counter may be, "Thank you, your Honor, but our expert's qualifications are actually part of our case." We judges do not want to be reversed on a claim that we foreclosed evidence crucial to a case.

Once qualifications are established, Federal Rule of Evidence 705 and most state rules allow you to mix and match the rest of the elements as you see fit. Gone are the days when you had to put questions in the form of a hypothetical or reveal all the underlying data before getting out the opinion.

With that said, it is still a good idea to give the jury some structure to follow. Headlines or signposting will aid the jurors in following complicated testimony. You may want to begin with, "Professor, I'm going to ask you: first, what you examined; second, what opinion you came to after that examination; third, why you believe that opinion is correct; and finally, where you differ from Professor X and why."

Time out for a style point. I like the phrase, "Tell us, Doctor, what is a comminuted fracture?" as opposed to, "Doctor, would you please tell the jury, what is a comminuted fracture?" The later version has the veiled message of, "Doctor, you and I know what a comminuted fracture is since we have many years of college after high school where we, by the way, did very well, but please Doctor, enlighten these poor schmucks!" Never underestimate a jury or even imply you are talking down to the jurors. "Tell us" is better than "Tell them."

The only exception I would make to this style point is on the actual opinion question. Experts are usually so expensive that I always liked to think that I was paying per question. Their name was a dollar, where they went to school was perhaps five dollars, but the opinion question was the hundred-dollar question. I wanted to put the opinion question in a frame, hang it on the wall, and put a spotlight on it.

So, the opinion question became a two-part question for emphasis. It went, "So, Doctor, do you have an opinion, to a reasonable degree of medical probability, as to the cause of Mr. Brown's seizures?" The expert answered, "Yes, I do," and my next question was, "Doctor, please tell the ladies and gentlemen of the jury your opinion." The phrase "ladies and gentlemen of the jury" is like calling a person by name. The jury pays attention, and, since it is an opinion question as opposed to a knowledge question, there is no danger of offending someone on the jury.

Sprinkled throughout your direct you may want to anticipate cross and build what some refer to as a "soft cross" into your own direct. For example, if your doctor looked only at the emergency room report to arrive at her opinion, you know she is going to be crossed on whether she has actually examined the plaintiff or even met the plaintiff for that matter.

You can anticipate this cross by a series of questions such as, "Now, Doctor, have you actually examined Mr. Simpson?" When she responds "No," you, with a bit of skepticism in your voice, ask, "Wouldn't it be important for you to actually examine the plaintiff?" Now I realize that this is a leading question. However, no one seems to ever object to it. The opposing lawyer never stands up and says, "Hey, wait a minute, you're doing my cross!" When the doctor responds that no, she does not actually need to examine the plaintiff to give this opinion, then it is a simple two-word question, "Why not?"

From this point on a good expert should carry the water for you. She might explain that it would be irrelevant to examine the plaintiff at this point in time since her assignment was only to give an opinion based upon what the plaintiff was presenting to the emergency room personnel on that day, at that time. A final note on this technique is that you must tell your expert the "soft cross" questions you will be asking on direct.

So now that we have a structure that is easy to follow, what else can we do to help the jury? I think your greatest role in the courtroom is that of the advocate, but I also believe your second greatest role is that of the teacher. I think juries tend to side with those attorneys who they perceive took the time, effort, and trouble to make a difficult area understandable.

If there is any way you can get the jury to see the opinion as well as hear the opinion, you will have a leg up. However, be sure the jurors know that you are the side that is making the case come alive through visuals. It goes something like this: "Doctor, have you brought anything to court with you today to aid us in understanding your opinions?" Your expert then says, "Yes, you asked me if I would scan in the records I looked at so we could show them to the jury." The jurors then sit up in anticipation of "seeing" the opinion come to life. Good luck.

Expert Cross: The "Islands" of Expert Opinion

I like to think of cross-examination of experts as two islands. There is "The Island of Expert Opinion," which is a very dangerous island. Then, there is "The Island of Everything Else," which is not as dangerous.

Every time I crossed an expert, my basic question was whether I was going to fight on the island of expert opinion or leave the fighting on that island to my own expert. For the most part, unless I could picture the other expert saying, "Oh, you're right, I'm wrong," I would tend not to go on his or her island. I would let my own expert fight on that island, and I would fight on the island of everything else.

I tell lawyers to be wary of advocacy advice that uses the words "always" or "never." So, I know there are some of you who may have advanced degrees in the opposing expert's area of expertise. You may have tried cases in one rather narrow area.

You feel entirely comfortable fighting them on their island. If you can go toe to toe on the expert's island, that's great. This article is for those who are a bit wary of fighting on the expert's island.

For those of you who do fight on the expert's island, I will give you a word of caution. Sometimes, when both the attorney and the expert are fighting back and forth on the opinion, they can leave the jury in the dust. I have seen these jargon-filled exchanges descend into two highly educated professionals going at each other with little regard for the people who are actually making the final decision. With that said, and for those who are wary of that island, let's take a closer look at the island of everything else.

To frame our discussion, I am going to pull quotes from a *Chicago Tribune* column written about the cross-examination of a Nobel Prize–winning expert. Now, if I knew that in one of my cases the other side had hired the winner of a Nobel Prize to oppose me, I would be somewhat intimidated.

However, after the cross, and before the defense presented any evidence, the judge directed a verdict in favor of the defendants. To be fair, his testimony covered 3 days for a total of 694 pages of transcript. Nevertheless, it appears from the article that what the columnist noted were all points made on the island of everything else.

> *"He admitted . . . that he worked just 40 hours in forming his basic opinions in the complex case against 24 manufacturers."*

What an Expert Doesn't Do

It is sometimes impossible, or not cost-effective, for experts to do everything. In a medical malpractice case, perhaps the only thing the other expert did was review records. While the expert may have an answer as to why he did not feel it necessary to actually examine the plaintiff, the fact that he never examined the plaintiff may score a point with the jury. Sometimes what an expert did not do is more important than what he did do.

> *"His 'research' amounted exclusively to reviewing documents provided by lawyers suing the drug companies."*

Source of Information

If all of the bases for his or her opinion comes from information from a biased source, that is an area for cross. Take a close look at the sources for the opinion. You may find a treasure trove of questions on sources that may have been better—or at least not as biased.

> *"He confessed that a paper he wrote supporting his opinion was so extensively rewritten by lawyers that no single original sentence survived intact."*

The Report

It doesn't get any better than that, does it? However, it is doubtful that you are going to have a case where the lawyers on the other side tinkered with every sentence in their own expert's report. So, let's dive deeper into the words in the actual report.

How many times does an expert use words such as "assume," "postulate," or "estimate"? Sometimes a good starting point is to ask the professor to go through the report and count and highlight every time one of those words is used in the report.

The expert report is like a chain that the expert is using to pull the jury toward his or her side. Any time the expert "assumes" a fact or figure, this can be a weak link in the chain.

Does the expert overuse, or even invent, jargon to try to sound like more of an expert? Some fringe experts make their reports more complicated and think complicated words make them more of an expert. Feed their words back to them and then try to put it in plain language for the jury. "Low coefficient of friction" really just means slippery. This can be fun.

Let's contrast another Nobel Prize winner, who could have given an opinion full of scientific gobbledygook, but instead modeled the genius of simplicity. At a press conference convened for the Challenger disaster, Dr. Richard Feynman simply placed O-ring material from the shuttle in a clamp and dropped it into his ice water. The material became rigid and dented. Dr. Feynman pulled it out of his glass and with simple understatement said, "I believe that has some significance for our problem."

> *"[He] barely examined a Congressional Budget Office report that debunked some of the significant arguments in the lawsuit."*

Learned Treatise

I am calling this "learned treatise." This actually may be on the expert's island, but I still classify this as safe since it uses the powerful tool of an authoritative source recognized by the court, which the expert must or should acknowledge.

Learn and know the exception for learned treatises under Federal Rule of Evidence 803(18), or if there is a rule comparable in your state. If you can lay a foundation that it is a reliable authority by the expert's own admission or even by your own expert's testimony, you can use it.

"Somehow his work totaled 300 hours, for a $180,000 paycheck."

Bias, Interest, or Prejudice

This expert was paid $600 per hour for his work. Does the expert have a monetary bias, a bias for testifying for only one side or for only one firm? If they usually testify for plaintiffs, have they ever once testified for the defense? Have they ever turned a case down? What percentage of their yearly income comes from court cases?

"Deeply ignorant."

Factual Basis

Does the expert have all the facts? Are there holes in her opinion or things she simply does not know? Do the groundwork in discovery so that you can probe these areas at trial. In addition, some experts are so high in the clouds that they won't dirty themselves by coming back to earth to learn and remember mundane things such as facts, dates, times, and people's names. Once again, this can be fun.

"And for two decades, [his] opinions paid off without his ever appearing on the stand."

Qualifications

Do your due diligence. The Internet has changed everything. Dig deep into the other expert's qualifications.

At my previous firm, one of the lawyers caught an expert on the other side lying about board certification. If you search for this expert's name on the Internet, you will find some background information. However, if you take the next step and type his name into any legal search engine, you will find an appellate court opinion where the concurring justice refers to the doctor as a "liar." Go one step further and type his name into our county website and you can find the perjury charge. Do your homework.

"He gave only a passing glance to the testimony of witnesses contradicting what he was about to say."

Your Expert

It has been my experience that good experts are rarely willing to attack the expert on the other side as being unqualified. I find doctors are particularly loath to attack other doctors on their credentials.

You can sometimes bolster you own expert by getting other experts to admit that they are not saying your doctor is a bad doctor or that she is unqualified. Many have referred patients back and forth or work at the same hospital. You can get them to admit your expert is qualified and their only disagreement is the opinion on this particular case.

Things Agreed Upon

I once heard a British barrister begin the cross of an expert with an elegant preface of "Professor, let us see if there is some common ground upon which we might agree." He then took the expert on a tour of his report as compared with the opposing expert's. The effect was to show that there was more agreement than disagreement on things such as the basic facts, some assumptions, and the approach to the calculations. As much as you can, use the other side's expert to bolster your own expert's report.

Resources:

David Greising, "His Testimony in Drug Case Deserves an F," *Chicago Tribune* (Dec. 2, 1998), *available at* http://bit.ly/drug-case.

Flynn v. Edmonds, 602 N.E.2d 880 (Ill. Ct. App. 4th Dist. 1992).

CHAPTER 5

PROFESSIONALISM

Small Steps That Lead to the Top

Being a Little Bit Better Is Often All You Need

Before I headed off to college, my father sat me down. In addition to some fatherly advice, he gave me a copy of *A Message to Garcia* by Elbert Hubbard. It was written at the turn of the century and the language is dated, but its message has withstood the test of time. It tells the story of a person who takes on a mission and runs with it. In my opinion, it contains what partners expect from their associates, judges expect from trial counsel, and clients expect from their lawyers.

Several years ago I was reading a book, the name of which escapes me. It had a sentence that stood out in the 200-odd pages. Since I cannot find the book, here's the gist: It is easy to get to the top as there is so little competition. Now, one would think in the highly competitive world of litigation this would not apply. However, my experience has been that you do not need to be twice as good as the next lawyer—you just need to be a little bit better. So, what are the little things that mean a lot? What is the road less traveled that made all the difference?

"What about a smile and saying 'thank you,'" offers Paul Mark Sandler, Baltimore, cochair of the Section of Litigation's Litigation Institute for Trial Training. Sandler's suggestion is simple and costs nothing, but its rewards can be great. I will tell you from experience that court personnel either like you, are neutral about you, or don't like you. If they really like you, they can help you. If they don't like you or ignore you, it shows.

The Advantage of Being Liked

Let me give some examples. Some attorneys stand in hallways and, with voices loud enough for anyone to hear, tell clients and witnesses what they are going or not going to do in court and what they are going or not going to offer. Some must believe this public posturing is a form of cheap advertising.

I have seen, and experienced, court personnel telling attorneys they like what they just heard in the hallway. They will not tell you this stuff if they do not like you. Attorneys who are not liked by court personnel run the risk of their conversations being repeated if they do not use the private conference rooms.

Let me be even more concrete. Over a decade ago, we had an out-of-town attorney come to court. At that time, Pauline's coffee shop was in the basement of the courthouse. Pauline was the chief cook and bottle washer. As a young attorney, I spent a lot of time there getting to know people, and I was usually there for morning coffee and lunch.

During the trial, this attorney would come in every morning and if Pauline was not at the counter, he would hit the counter with his hand to get her attention and say something like "Hey, can we get some coffee out here? We've got to be in court." Pauline loathed the man. You know where the jurors ate lunch? He lost the case. I cannot say he lost the case due to Pauline running him down the entire lunch hour, but I'm sure it did not help.

If you're still not convinced, let me share this story of how just one statement by a bailiff changed jury trials in our courthouse. One jury term we suddenly noticed a spike in questions from the jury. In most cases, we would get no questions, or at most, one or two. With some juries, we were now getting upwards of 10 questions per jury. We tracked this down to a new bailiff who, as he was shutting the door to the jury room, would say, "And if you have any questions at all, the judge would be glad to answer them." That one sentence changed their behavior.

Social scientists say that it only takes a matter of seconds for a person to view an interaction between two other people and assess whether they like each other or not. How the court personnel, bailiffs, court reporters, and clerks relate to you in a courtroom speaks volumes to those jurors.

The jurors look to the court personnel for information and guidance on a variety of issues, such as when they can make calls or which way to the bathroom. Treat the court personnel well, smile, thank them, learn their names, and you will never have to worry about how jurors perceive you.

Attorneys on Trial

Let's turn to the trial. Attorneys seem to forget that court reporters only have two hands. Some are astonished when court reporters get irritated with them while they talk at the same time they ask for an exhibit to be marked. Clerks also get irritated if attorneys depend on them to find their exhibits in the pile or remind them which number they are on.

"Always pull every exhibit that you intend to use with a witness in the courtroom from the clerk's file before the witness takes the stand," says Don Bivens, Phoenix, Chair-elect of the ABA Section of Litigation. "Have them in front of the witness in the correct order. You will look more professional, everyone will appreciate your efficiency, and it allows you to tell your story without the interruption of trying to find each new exhibit in the clerk's pile."

With the exception of perhaps the wheel and the lightbulb, I believe the three-ring binder is our greatest invention. I despise those big, black metal clips used to hold loose documents. I believe some attorneys must hire Russian Olympic weightlifters to hold the clips open so as many documents as possible can be crammed into the grip of the clip.

Papers literally explode from the stack once I free them from their bondage. Why must I free them? No one can read the top two inches of any document when these clips are used. No normal human being can ever get the documents back into the clip. Just so you know, I feel the same way about large rubber bands as document containment devices.

Judges love three-ring binders. "We often make exhibit binders for the jury as well," advises Judge Lorna G. Schofield, New York, U.S. District Judge for the Southern District of New York and past chair of the Section. "That way the jury has the ease of referring to the exhibits in the same way the judge does. When I am arguing to the bench, I always bring the entire case, highlight the relevant portion, and give a copy to both the judge and my adversary so I am never accused of withholding the entire case."

"Something I did as an associate, which I considered at the time to be a small thing, I think made a huge difference in my becoming a partner," continues Schofield. "I wrote a memo where I analyzed the facts, deduced a theory, but, in addition, I attached all of the supporting documents with exhibit tabs in a way you might do for a court, although it was just an internal memo for the partner. This seemed to surprise and wow everyone."

You, as trial counsel, should love three-ring binders for a purely selfish reason. Not only do they appeal to the people who are deciding your cases, but they also help you organize your trial. You never lose an exhibit on your desk.

If you then go the extra mile and prepare exhibit binders for everyone in the courtroom, it eliminates the exhibit dance of having to ask permission to approach, marking the exhibit, showing it to opposing counsel, showing it to the witness, and so on. When the case is over, you can get them back and use them again for the next trial. You may then, and only then, bind those exhibits with one of those big, black metal clips before you throw them in storage.

Visuals for the Jury

Tweaking your presentation of visuals for the jury can make a big difference as well. "When drawing or writing numbers on a white pad, have the sketch or numbers very lightly drawn—visible only when close—in advance," suggests Bivens. "People will be amazed how quickly and perfectly you can put things on the board and will watch closely every time you do put something on the board."

"When presenting a key part of an exhibit on a large screen, don't simply throw the excerpt on the screen," counsels Bivens. "No one knows where it came from or who wrote it. Show the front page first, then perhaps the relevant signatures, then highlight the key language. It can be done in a matter of seconds, but gives you the advantage of putting things in context and reminding the decision makers that the parties signed this agreement."

Finally, to put everything in perspective, we will end with a little story about sand. "The most moving travel experience I've had was visiting the D-Day beaches in Normandy," says Steven O. Rosen, Portland, OR, cochair of the Section's Legal Services Training Committee. "A year later a friend also visited the beaches and brought back to me a small jar of sand that he filled on Omaha Beach. That sand reminds me that whatever task, deadline, or feared adverse consequences may be, those things are manageable and not all that bad. The sand always keeps me going."

Dealing with Jerks: What Goes Around Comes Around

Name-calling is unprofessional, I know. But to quote Mark Twain, "The difference between the almost right word and the right word is really a large matter—it's the difference between the lightning bug and the lightning." "Jerk" is the right word, but by "jerk" I mean those (thankfully) few attorneys for whom getting under their adversary's skin seems more important than the result they achieve for their client. You should also know that "jerk" is my word. No one quoted in this article ever used that word to describe an opponent.

So let us begin, and let us begin with you. A proverb found in Luke says, "Physician, heal thyself." Counsel, heal thyself. Your attitude and how you approach this issue is everything.

You signed up for this duty. No one put a gun to your head and forced you to pick trial work. If you wanted peace and quiet, you should be drafting wills for a living. I know you would like it if everyone were as reasonable as you, but once you accept the fact that you have picked an area of law that possibly contains the greatest concentration of jerks, you'll be in a much better frame of mind. Jerks come with the territory. Confrontation is like oxygen to some attorneys. Live with it.

Next, let's turn to the jerk. To the pure jerk, the fight is more important than the result he achieves for his client. As they say in Texas, "He's all hat, no cattle."

I believe that, as a general rule, jerks are not as successful as those attorneys who keep their eye on the prize. Watch any successful trial lawyer and you will see single-minded focus on the end result. Very little time is wasted in side battles with opposing counsel simply for the sake of the side battle.

One final note on this topic: Beware the billable hour. If the attorney is getting paid by the hour, he or she gets paid just as much money for time expended being a jerk, or spending time dealing with a jerk, as he or she does on hours spent seeking a good result. Those attorneys who are paid based upon the result, rather than the hour, tend to have the single-minded focus of which I speak. For them, fighting with counsel on tangential matters simply does not pay.

General Rules for Dealing with Jerks

Now that we've addressed your general mindset, let's turn to some experts for the specifics. Weighing in on this subject will be two former cochairs for the Section's Ethics and Professionalism Committee—Gregory R. Hanthorn, Atlanta, and Craig C. Martin, Chicago, along with Anne Marie Seibel, Birmingham, AL, former cochair of The Woman Advocate Committee, and Laura H. Kennedy, Phoenix, former cochair of The Young Advocates Committee.

"I have an alternating series of do's and don'ts," suggests Hanthorn. "First, don't respond in kind. Bad behavior from someone else does not obligate me to behave unprofessionally."

"Don't rise to the bait," agrees Seibel. "I once was complimented by a senior partner on how I handled a very agitated and very bitter witness on cross by keeping a very even tone and being professional. I think this [is] similar. They're doing it to get a reaction out of you, and to continue to be calm, cool and collected is a way of showing that they can't get under your skin."

"Do consider dropping your own volume as your adversary raises his or hers," continues Hanthorn. "It's amazing how often having to slow down to listen leads to softer, slower speech by all involved."

Jerks are sometimes simply performing under the (usually mistaken) belief that this behavior impresses clients. If the clients are also jerks, that may be true, but getting the jerk one-on-one, without the client, may help. You may find that you can make far more headway with an adversary if you meet him or her in private, at a neutral place, where he or she cannot play to an audience.

Jerks in Depositions

Depositions are prime opportunities for jerks to perform—at least those jerks who are oblivious to how they are coming across to judges or juries. "My sense is to follow the Golden Rule and treat them the way you would want to be treated," says Martin. "Second, I find that a well-prepared client is much more able to deal with a difficult lawyer taking a deposition than is the lawyer defending the deposition. For example, there are some lawyers who like to show clients documents that have nothing to do with the case. It is much more effective if the client can say they have never seen that document before and hands it back to the lawyer rather than the defender making objections all over the record about how the witness has never seen the document before."

"As far as your preparation to deal with someone acting like a jerk, you need to be more prepared than they are," counsels Kennedy. "I would add you need to be more prepared than you think you need to be, because this puts you in a better position to either ignore them or gives you the confidence to fight back. When you are that well prepared, you can deal with them without worrying about your case, and it allows you to concentrate on substance of the case and what you need to do for your client."

Know Thy Enemy

You'll be doing yourself and your client a favor by finding out as much as you can about opposing counsel and how they operate. Once you know the cases they have worked on, you can call friends and colleagues to find out whether they are true professionals. Handling jerks is much easier for you and your client if you know in advance what to expect.

If you find out early that the person on the other side may not be the consummate professional, you may want to try and reach some preliminary agreements before things heat up. In *The Last Thirty Days Before Trial*, former member of the Section's Trial Advisory Board Stephen D. Susman, Houston, has crafted a checklist of 15 pretrial agreements that can be used at the beginning of the case to eliminate controversies and save costs on both sides.

Restraint in Writing

Let's turn to written communication. Emails often have a deleterious effect on professional courtesy. People will say things in emails that they would never say to a person face to face. "Sometimes it is worth picking up the telephone and actually cutting through whatever the issues are," counsels Martin. "If that doesn't work and I am working with a large team, I have told a difficult adversary that they will have a single point of contact at our firm and it's not going to be me. I then assign someone on our team who has the time and capacity and tenacity to deal with that person."

"With regard to emails, don't fire back an emotional response," suggests Hanthorn. "Take time to confirm facts and include facts. Do assume your emails and letters will eventually become exhibits to a motion. Don't accept what I label 'book or record of the month emails' where they say unless they receive a response they assume you agree. Do ask them to please not send you any more communications that imply no response is agreement."

It's What You Do When No One Is Watching

Character has been defined as what we do when we think that no one is watching. Always, always, always assume that a judge or a jury will eventually see how you both behaved either by way of emails, letters, transcripts, or even more devastating, a video deposition. There is no downside to taking the high road. Remember, if you wrestle with a pig, all that happens is that you both get muddy—but only the pig enjoys it.

Many jerks start fights just to see how you will respond and whether you will respond in kind. They hate silence, and they hate it when you don't lower yourself to their level. Don't interrupt them, let them exhaust their bile and, trust me, the judge or, better yet, the jury will have the last word on their behavior. There is nothing more satisfying than seeing the jurors' reactions when counsel, who was downright unctuous in jury selection, shows their true colors in a videotaped deposition. Unless the judge allows editing worthy of a Hollywood movie, it is hard to edit out all the bad behavior.

Finally, I believe the single quality that separates people from other creatures is their ability to remember the past and learn from it—and their ability to see into the future for a period of more than five seconds. In the practice of law, this means that every person an attorney encounters is either a potential client or a possible referral for a potential client, even if he or she is on the other side of the case.

But when it comes to perspective, jerks tend to be myopic. "We've had cases where we took the deposition of a corporate officer at a decision-making level where opposing counsel was difficult to deal with," recalls Hanthorn. "Then, within a few months after the matter was resolved, we were approached and ultimately engaged by that same corporation."

As I tell people in court, if you want to be biblical about it, as you sow so shall you reap. If you want to be scientific about it, for every action there is an equal and opposite reaction. If you want to be colloquial, what goes around, comes around.

Resources:

The Last Thirty Days Before Trial is available for free to all members of the Section at www.americanbar.org/content/dam/aba/migrated/litigation/mo/premium-lt/prog_materials/teleconferences/0108_thirtydays.authcheckdam.pdf .

Never Give Up

You Never Know When the Tide Might Turn

He was a legend in the local bar. If you walked into a meeting and saw him holding court there, you could pretty much be assured of having a good conversation and a good time.

He always said, "If I had known I was going to live this long, I would have taken much better care of myself." Apropos of that, I once went to his office and noticed a pack of Pall Mall non-filtered cigarettes next to a pack of filtered Marlboros.

I asked, "After all these years of smoking, you still can't decide?" His face lit up and with the air of a reformed addict said, "Oh that's my smoking reduction plan. I alternate smoking a non-filtered Pall Mall, which I really prefer, with a filtered Marlboro, which is much better for my health." That was R. P., and it was R. P. who gave me a lesson in not giving up.

When I was first appointed, I was assigned to traffic court. At that time, R. P. had to be close to 70 years old. One morning he walks into the 8:30 city traffic call. I was a bit surprised since he rarely handled a case that small. I opened the file, and in it there was his motion for summary judgment on a failure to yield to the right at an open intersection case—an ordinance violation. The fine was $85.

The city code lists each intersection in the city where one is required to yield to the right. Evidently, the person who drafted the code had simply missed one of the intersections. It just happened to be the intersection where R.P.'s client was cited.

Both the city attorney and I scrambled for the city code and, true enough, the intersection had been missed. The city attorney conceded the motion, and after the case was dismissed, the following occurred:

> Me: Counsel, one does not usually see this level of lawyering at 8:30 in the morning on an $85 city ordinance ticket.

R. P.: Your Honor, I start at square one.

Me: Well, this is a highly personal question, you don't have to answer it, but what would one charge a client for this level of lawyering at 8:30 in the morning on an $85 dollar city ordinance ticket?

And R. P., with a glint in his eye, a smile on his face, and an actor's timing, responded, "Your Honor . . . I usually . . . just add . . . a zero."

Pursue When Worthy

So what do I mean by the admonition "Never give up"? What I am not talking about are cases that should be settled either due to bad facts or client concerns. What I am talking about are cases that you and your client have decided are worth pursuing.

Harriet Beecher Stowe probably put it best when she said, "When you get into a tight place and everything goes against you, till it seems as though you could not hang on a minute longer, never give up then, for that is just the place and time that the tide will turn."

"My story about never giving up involves my very first civil jury trial," recalls Charles S. Fax, Bethesda, MD, associate editor of *Litigation News*. "I represented the plaintiff, an African American woman, who claimed that she had been denied an apartment because of her race. She had no financial resources, and I took the case on a flyer. I sent in testers and achieved a positive result, but the evidence was circumstantial."

"I issued massive discovery requests and got reams of rental data and so forth, but its utility—in terms of isolating the key issue of racial discrimination—was limited at best," relates Fax. "Finally I asked for the names and addresses of former property managers, figuring they might have something to tell me. I got a list of names and addresses, but they were all quite dated. I mailed out a form letter to the last known address of each person listed, asking them to contact me. No one did. That was four or five months before trial."

"I prepared for trial in the expectation that my client's testimony, combined with the circumstantial evidence, might be enough to get me to the jury, but that a conservative jury, as Virginia juries were back then, would be inclined to reach a defense verdict," recounts Fax. "Two days before trial, my secretary tells me that there is a call for me from Alaska. The woman on the phone tells me that she was a former property manager at the apartment and she had received a letter from me, which had been forwarded twice."

"I asked her whether she could shed any light on the landlord's rental practices and she responded, 'I thought that might be why you were calling and, yes, I can. The landlord always instructed me never to rent to 'Blacks, Jews, or hippies,'" relates Fax. "I asked her to hold, ran to my managing partner's office, and practically shouted, 'Can we pay for round-trip airfare from Alaska?' He responded with two words, 'Do it.'"

"We flew her in that night and put her up at a motel around the corner from the courthouse," continues Fax. "Of course, she was not on our witness list, but I laid the foundation in my cross-examination of the landlord and then called her as a rebuttal witness. I can tell you that my greatest satisfaction was not in achieving a verdict for the plaintiff, but rather, in observing the landlord's panicked reaction when he realized who she was as she entered the courtroom."

Inspirational Examples

It is only fitting that I write this column during the year that celebrates the 50th anniversary of *Gideon v. Wainwright*. Clarence Earl Gideon is perhaps the best example, and best inspiration in our legal world, of a person who never gave up. On November 11, 1963, then Attorney General Robert F. Kennedy said, "If an obscure Florida convict named Clarence Earl Gideon had not sat down in prison with a pencil and paper to write a letter to the Supreme Court, and if the Supreme Court had not taken the trouble to look for merit in that one crude petition among all the bundles of mail it must receive every day, the vast machinery of American law would have gone on functioning undisturbed."

Another compelling story of never giving up is in the book, *Contempt of Court*, by Mark Curriden and Leroy Phillips Jr. A black man is accused of raping a white woman in Tennessee in the early 1900s. White lawyers did their best to defend at trial, but he was convicted by an all-white jury.

Two black lawyers take up the case and secure a stay of execution from the U.S. Supreme Court. He is lynched in his jail cell, and the rest of the story surrounds the criminal trial in which the Supreme Court found the local officials in contempt of court for allowing the lynching to take place.

A Father Who Didn't Give Up

I will end with a story of my own. In the early 1990s, I represented a father who opposed the mother moving with their minor child from Illinois to Washington, D.C. The mother alleged she was getting remarried and her new husband could only find a job in that area.

The father alleged that the marriage was a ruse to interfere with his visitation and increase the mother's chances of success in her petition to remove the minor child. The father claimed that one of the motivations for the move was animosity towards him.

The trial court allowed the move in 1991. The father appealed, and the decision was affirmed in 1992, with one judge dissenting. The father then filed a petition for leave to appeal to the Illinois Supreme Court, which was denied in 1993. A denial by the highest court in the state is usually the end of the story. However, the father did not give up.

In 1994, the father filed a petition with the trial court, alleging that within weeks after the Illinois Supreme Court denied his petition, the mother separated from her husband. He alleged that a fraud had been committed on the trial court and that the mother's marriage was a ruse to frustrate his visitation.

So, in the words of Paul Harvey, here's the rest of the story. In the November 24, 2003, issue of *Sports Illustrated* under the column "*Faces in the Crowd*," you will find this entry: "Adam Pfeiffer, golf. Adam, a senior at Quincy Senior High, won the class AA state high school golf championship at The Den at Fox Creek in Bloomington. His two-day combined score of 143 is the lowest in the 28-year history of the event." Quincy and Bloomington are cities in the state of Illinois.

Resources:

The 50th Anniversary of Gideon v. Wainwright, ABA Section of Litigation, Live Streaming Events, Section of Litigation.

Mark Curriden and Leroy Phillips Jr., *Contempt of Court: The Turn-of-the-Century Lynching That Launched a Hundred Years of Federalism*, Faber & Faber, 1999, ISBN: 0-385-72082-3. *See also* American Bar Association Criminal Justice Section, *Criminal Justice Magazine*.
Pfeiffer v. Pfeiffer, 604 N.E.2d 1069 (3rd Dist. Ill. 1992).

CREDITS

Trial Preparation

"The Trial Notebook: Nuts and Bolts of Trial Preparation," by Mark Drummond. ©2009. Published in *Litigation News*, Volume 34, Issue 3, by the American Bar Association. Reproduced with permission. All rights reserved. This information or any portion thereof may not be copied or disseminated in any form or by any means or stored in an electronic database or retrieval system without the express written consent of the American Bar Association or the copyright holder.

"Tigar on Trials . . . and Life: Information, Instruction, and Inspiration," by Mark Drummond. ©2010. Published in *Litigation News*, Volume 33, Issue 2, by the American Bar Association. Reproduced with permission. All rights reserved. This information or any portion thereof may not be copied or disseminated in any form or by any means or stored in an electronic database or retrieval system without the express written consent of the American Bar Association or the copyright holder.

"Working Backward from the Appeal," by Mark Drummond. ©2011. Published in *Litigation News*, Volume 36, Issue 4, by the American Bar Association. Reproduced with permission. All rights reserved. This information or any portion thereof may not be copied or disseminated in any form or by any means or stored in an electronic database or retrieval system without the express written consent of the American Bar Association or the copyright holder.

"Know Thy Judge," by Mark Drummond. ©2008. Published in *Litigation News*, Volume 34, Issue 1, by the American Bar Association. Reproduced with permission. All rights reserved. This information or any portion thereof may not be copied or disseminated in any form or by any means or stored in an electronic database or retrieval system without the express written consent of the American Bar Association or the copyright holder.

"What Judges Want," by Mark Drummond. ©2005. Published in Litigation, Volume 31, Issue 4, by the American Bar Association. Reproduced with permission. All rights reserved. This information or any portion thereof may not be copied or disseminated in any form or by any means or stored in an electronic database or retrieval system without the express written consent of the American Bar Association or the copyright holder.

Jury Selection

"Bloggers, Bailouts & the Economy," by Mark Drummond. ©2010. Published in *Litigation News*, Volume 35, Issue 4, by the American Bar Association. Reproduced with permission. All rights reserved. This information or any portion thereof may not be copied or disseminated in any form or by any means or stored in an electronic database or retrieval system without the express written consent of the American Bar Association or the copyright holder.

"Implicit Bias Can Be Eliminated by Awareness," by Mark Drummond. ©2011. Published in *Litigation News*, Volume 36, Issue 3, by the American Bar Association. Reproduced with permission. All rights reserved. This information or any portion thereof may not be copied or disseminated in any form or by any means or stored in an electronic database or retrieval system without the express written consent of the American Bar Association or the copyright holder.

"Don't Let the Judge Cut You Out," by Mark Drummond. ©2012. Published in *Litigation News*, Volume 37, Issue 3, by the American Bar Association. Reproduced with permission. All rights reserved. This information or any portion thereof may not be copied or disseminated in any form or by any means or stored in an electronic database or retrieval system without the express written consent of the American Bar Association or the copyright holder.

"A Peer May Be Your Client's Worst Juror," by Mark Drummond. ©2012. Published in *Litigation News*, Volume 37, Issue 4, by the

American Bar Association. Reproduced with permission. All rights reserved. This information or any portion thereof may not be copied or disseminated in any form or by any means or stored in an electronic database or retrieval system without the express written consent of the American Bar Association or the copyright holder.

"How About a Free Shadow Jury? Inside the Juror's Mind," by Mark Drummond. ©2013. Published in *Litigation News*, Volume 38, Issue 2, by the American Bar Association. Reproduced with permission. All rights reserved. This information or any portion thereof may not be copied or disseminated in any form or by any means or stored in an electronic database or retrieval system without the express written consent of the American Bar Association or the copyright holder.

Trial Presentation

"Brain Science for the Courtroom: Tips for Attention and Retention," by Mark Drummond. ©2009. Published in *Litigation News*, Volume 35, Issue 1, by the American Bar Association. Reproduced with permission. All rights reserved. This information or any portion thereof may not be copied or disseminated in any form or by any means or stored in an electronic database or retrieval system without the express written consent of the American Bar Association or the copyright holder.

"Handling the Bad Stuff in Court," by Mark Drummond. ©2010. Published in *Litigation News*, Volume 36, Issue 1, by the American Bar Association. Reproduced with permission. All rights reserved. This information or any portion thereof may not be copied or disseminated in any form or by any means or stored in an electronic database or retrieval system without the express written consent of the American Bar Association or the copyright holder.

"Acting in Court. If All the World's a Stage, What's Court?," by Mark Drummond. ©2011. Published in *Litigation News*, Volume 37, Issue 1, by the American Bar Association. Reproduced with permission. All rights reserved. This information or any portion thereof may not be copied or disseminated in any form or by any means or stored in an electronic database or retrieval system without the express written consent of the American Bar Association or the copyright holder.

"Lessons from a Luddite: Top 10 Tips for Visuals," by Mark Drummond. ©2013. Published in *Litigation News*, Volume 39, Issue 1, by the American Bar Association. Reproduced with permission. All rights reserved. This information or any portion thereof may not be copied or disseminated in any form or by any means or stored in an electronic database or retrieval system without the express written consent of the American Bar Association or the copyright holder.

"The Power of Simplicity," by Mark Drummond. ©2014. Published in *Litigation News*, Volume 39, Issue 3, by the American Bar Association. Reproduced with permission. All rights reserved. This information or any portion thereof may not be copied or disseminated in any form or by any means or stored in an electronic database or retrieval system without the express written consent of the American Bar Association or the copyright holder.

"Is Technology Changing Our Brains?," by Mark Drummond. ©2014. Published in Litigation News, Volume 40, Issue 3, by the American Bar Association. Reproduced with permission. All rights reserved. This information or any portion thereof may not be copied or disseminated in any form or by any means or stored in an electronic database or retrieval system without the express written consent of the American Bar Association or the copyright holder.

Witness Examination

"Panning for Gold: A Depositions Roundtable," by Mark Drummond. ©2010. Published in *Litigation News*, Volume 35, Issue 3, by the American Bar Association. Reproduced with permission. All rights reserved. This information or any portion thereof may not be copied or disseminated in any form or by any means or stored in an electronic database or retrieval system without the express written consent of the American Bar Association or the copyright holder.

"Thinking Ahead on Impeachment," by Mark Drummond. ©2009. Published in *Litigation News*, Volume 34, Issue 4, by the American Bar Association. Reproduced with permission. All rights reserved. This information or any portion thereof may not be copied or disseminated in any form or by any means or stored in an electronic database or retrieval system without the express written consent of the American Bar Association or the copyright holder.

"Defending Depositions. Know the Rules: Written and Unwritten," by Mark Drummond. ©2011. Published in *Litigation News*, Volume 36, Issue 2, by the American Bar Association. Reproduced with permission. All rights reserved. This information or any portion thereof may not be copied or disseminated in any form or by any means or stored in an electronic database or retrieval system without the express written consent of the American Bar Association or the copyright holder.

"Sometimes It Pays to Be Underestimated. How to Do an Effective Cross Without Resorting to Rambo Tactics," by Mark Drummond and Peter Lyons. ©2014. Published in *Litigation News*, Volume 39, Issue 2, by the American Bar Association. Reproduced with permission. All rights reserved. This information or any portion thereof may not be copied or disseminated in any form or by any means or stored in an electronic database or retrieval system without the express written consent of the American Bar Association or the copyright holder.

"Making Experts Come Alive," by Mark Drummond. ©2014. Published in *Litigation News*, Volume 39, Issue 4, by the American Bar Association. Reproduced with permission. All rights reserved. This information or any portion thereof may not be copied or disseminated in any form or by any means or stored in an electronic database or retrieval system without the express written consent of the American Bar Association or the copyright holder.

"Expert Cross: The 'Islands' of Expert Opinion," by Mark Drummond. ©2014. Published in *Litigation News*, Volume 40, Issue 1, by the

American Bar Association. Reproduced with permission. All rights reserved. This information or any portion thereof may not be copied or disseminated in any form or by any means or stored in an electronic database or retrieval system without the express written consent of the American Bar Association or the copyright holder.

Professionalism

"Small Steps That Lead to the Top," by Mark Drummond. ©2012. Published in *Litigation News*, Volume 38, Issue 1, by the American Bar Association. Reproduced with permission. All rights reserved. This information or any portion thereof may not be copied or disseminated in any form or by any means or stored in an electronic database or retrieval system without the express written consent of the American Bar Association or the copyright holder.

"Dealing with Jerks: What Goes Around Comes Around," by Mark Drummond. ©2011. Published in *Litigation News*, Volume 37, Issue 1, by the American Bar Association. Reproduced with permission. All rights reserved. This information or any portion thereof may not be copied or disseminated in any form or by any means or stored in an electronic database or retrieval system without the express written consent of the American Bar Association or the copyright holder.

"Never Give Up," by Mark Drummond. ©2012. Published in *Litigation News*, Volume 38, Issue 3, by the American Bar Association. Reproduced with permission. All rights reserved. This information or any portion thereof may not be copied or disseminated in any form or by any means or stored in an electronic database or retrieval system without the express written consent of the American Bar Association or the copyright holder.

INDEX